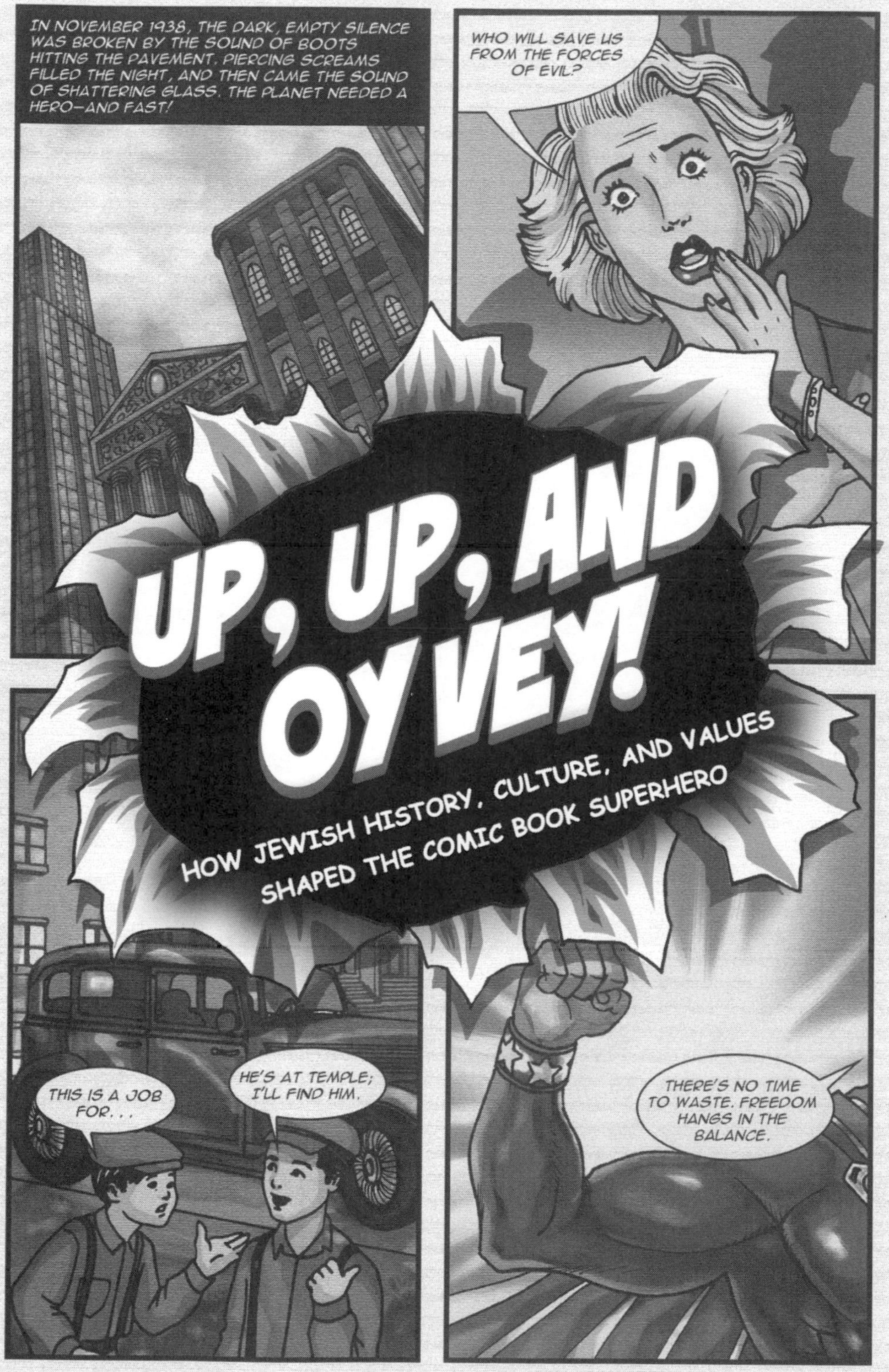
IN NOVEMBER 1938, THE DARK, EMPTY SILENCE WAS BROKEN BY THE SOUND OF BOOTS HITTING THE PAVEMENT. PIERCING SCREAMS FILLED THE NIGHT, AND THEN CAME THE SOUND OF SHATTERING GLASS. THE PLANET NEEDED A HERO—AND FAST!
WHO WILL SAVE US FROM THE FORCES OF EVIL?
UP, UP, AND OY VEY!
HOW JEWISH HISTORY, CULTURE, AND VALUES SHAPED THE COMIC BOOK SUPERHERO
THIS IS A JOB FOR. . .
HE'S AT TEMPLE; I'LL FIND HIM.
THERE'S NO TIME TO WASTE. FREEDOM HANGS IN THE BALANCE.

UP, UP, AND OY VEY!

HOW JEWISH HISTORY, CULTURE, AND VALUES SHAPED THE COMIC BOOK SUPERHERO

SIMCHA WEINSTEIN

leviathan press™

wisdom for the mind, inspiration for the soul™

Leviathan Press
25 Hooks Lane, Suite 202
Baltimore, Maryland 21208
(410) 653-0300
http://www.leviathanpress.com

Notice of Rights

Cataloging-in-Publication Data

Weinstein, Simcha, 1975-
   Up, up and oy vey! : how Jewish history, culture, and values shaped the comic book superhero / Simcha Weinstein. -- 1st ed. --
   p. ; cm.
Includes bibliographical references and index.
ISBN-13: 978-1-881927-32-7
ISBN-10: 1-881927-32-6
   1. Comic books, strips, etc.--History--Jewish influences. 2. Comic books, strips, etc.--History and criticism. 3. Comic books, strips, etc.--Social aspects. 4. Comic strip characters--History. 5. Heroes in literature--History. 6. Jews in popular culture. 7. Jews in literature. I. Title.
PN6710 .W45 2006
741.509--dc22   0606

PRINTED IN THE UNITED STATES OF AMERICA

Cover design and page layout by Rahel Block.
Copyedit by PeopleSpeak.
Index by Rachel Rice.

Distributed to the trade by Biblio Distribution
        (800) 462-6420   http://www.bibliodistribution.com

Distributed to Judaica booksellers by Judaica Press
        (800) 972-6201   http://www.judaicapress.com

All books from Leviathan Press are available at bulk order discounts for educational, promotional, and fund-raising purposes. For information call (800) LEVIATHAN.

For Ariella, Mendel, and Eli

Where there are no leaders, strive to be a leader.
—Ethics of the Fathers

You don't have to make a speech, big shot!
We understand! We've gotta use that power to help mankind, right?
—The Thing

Table of Contents

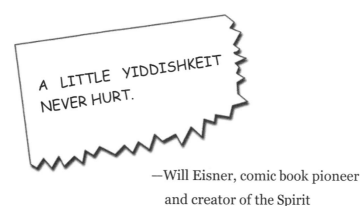

A LITTLE YIDDISHKEIT NEVER HURT.

—Will Eisner, comic book pioneer
and creator of the Spirit

For most of my life, I lived a Clark Kent existence: that of a Jew living in Manchester, England, intent on blending into the modern, secular world. I kept my Hebrew name a closely guarded secret. My desire to assimilate required no less.

I shrugged off Jewish ritual as spiritual Valium, something other people needed to escape the responsibilities of life. My idea of religious observance was limited to wolfing down bagels and lox while watching a *Seinfeld* rerun. I schlepped to a Passover Seder every year, but the celebration held little significance for me. My lifelong passion (or, dare I say, religion) was popular culture and its heroes: Spider-Man, Indiana Jones, James Bond.

My passion led to a degree in film history and a job scouting movie locations. I mingled with the bold and the beautiful, yet something was missing. When the reality behind my dreams turned out to be a disappointment, I realized I had nothing real and true to fall back on.

Seeking to fulfill needs that were not met by MTV and materialism, I set out to meet my great-great-grandparents and finally learn about my Jewish heritage. Would the skullcap I'd dropped along the road to assimilation still fit? To my surprise and relief, it did. Trips to Israel followed. Then I enrolled in Yeshiva (a Jewish learning institute).

As it turned out, all the excitement and inspiration that movies once represented to me were also contained within Judaism, and then some. I reverted to my Hebrew name (from Simon to Simcha, the Hebrew word for "joy") and with that I embraced my true inner essence, my real identity.

Yet I never lost my love of pop culture entirely. Marriage brought me to New York City, where I began thinking about all the Jewish writers, artists, and editors who'd lived and worked there in the 1930s and 1940s—and who'd created a whole new art form: the comic book. Why, I wondered, had the comic book been invented in that particular time and place by those particular men? Now, as a rabbi, I started rereading classic superhero comics from a whole new perspective: through the lens of Jewish tradition and spiritual belief.

This book represents my discoveries.

Acknowledgments

I'd like to thank the following people for their support, encouragement, generosity, and candor:

- The countless comic book writers and artists who continue to stretch my imagination.
- The amazing team at Leviathan Press: Jen Stein, Dr. Paul Volosov, Rahel Block, and Shimon Apisdorf. (Isn't it ironic that I was reading your books all those years ago and now I've written one?)
- Sharon Goldinger, my wonderful editor, who makes my words understandable.
- Kathy Shaidle, who fights for truth, justice, and the American way, one blog at a time.
- Steven M. Bergson, librarian at the Jewish Public Library of Toronto and a respected comic book historian. I am grateful for your extraordinary perception and valuable editorial suggestions.
- Rivka Jacobs, the world's number one Magneto fan.

- Stan "the Man" Lee, a real mensch.
- The wonderful folks at Congregation B'nai Avraham, Brooklyn Heights.
- Rabbis Benjamin Blech, Shlomo Gestetner, DovBer Pinson, Aaron L. Raskin, and Daniel Rowe—very wise dudes indeed!
- George and Pamela Rohr, who make sure that Jewish students across the world are aware of their superbackground.
- My students, who trash my apartment every Friday night—may it continue for many years.
- The true superheroes: my holy brothers and sisters at Chabad on Campus, who provide a home away from home for tens of thousands of Jewish students. You are truly the Rebbe's army.
- My dear friends and family on the other side of the pond in Manchester, England, who continue to be there for me—even though I have a beard.
- My dear brother David, parents, parents-in-law, and Nanny—I thank you for your support and belief in all my crazy antics.
- My darling dynamic duo, Mendel and Eli. I love you guys very much, even if you don't sleep.
- Ariella, my very own wonder woman. Thank you for raising our children while their daddy was busy reading comic books.

INTRODUCTION: PEOPLE OF THE (COMIC) BOOK

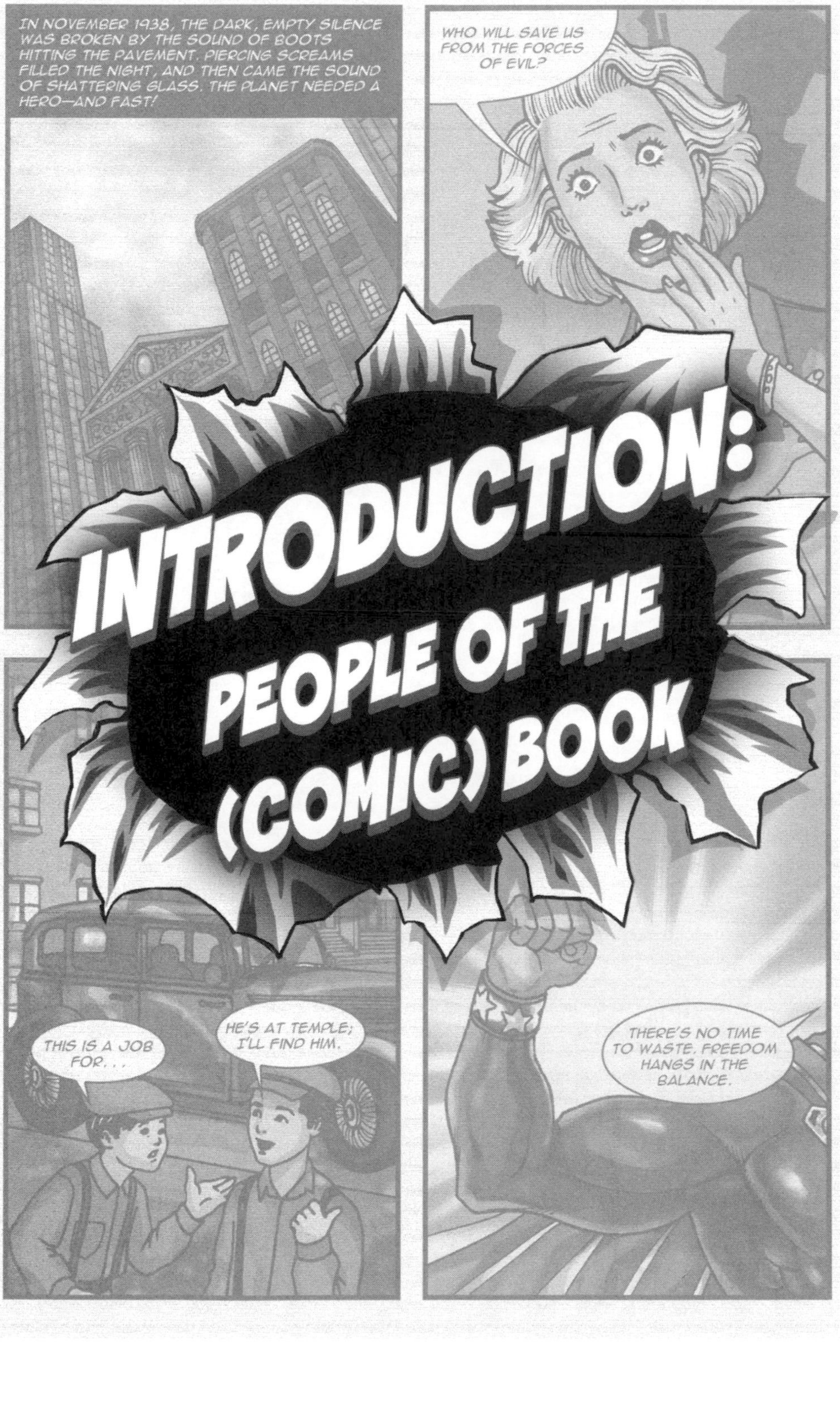

IN NOVEMBER 1938, THE DARK, EMPTY SILENCE WAS BROKEN BY THE SOUND OF BOOTS HITTING THE PAVEMENT. PIERCING SCREAMS FILLED THE NIGHT, AND THEN CAME THE SOUND OF SHATTERING GLASS. THE PLANET NEEDED A HERO—AND FAST!
WHO WILL SAVE US FROM THE FORCES OF EVIL?
THIS IS A JOB FOR. . .
HE'S AT TEMPLE; I'LL FIND HIM.
THERE'S NO TIME TO WASTE. FREEDOM HANGS IN THE BALANCE.

IT MAY NOT BE TRUE IN ALL CASES, BUT IT'S A PRETTY GOOD RULE OF THUMB. IF THE WORD "MAN" APPEARS AT THE END OF SOMEONE'S NAME YOU CAN DRAW ONE OF TWO CONCLUSIONS: A) THEY'RE JEWISH, AS IN GOLDMAN, FELDMAN OR LIPMAN; OR B) THEY'RE A SUPERHERO, AS IN SUPERMAN, BATMAN OR SPIDER-MAN.

—Zeddy Lawrence, television writer,
Dream Team

Before Superman, Batman, and Spider-Man, there were the superpatriarchs and supermatriarchs of the Bible and heroic figures named Moses, Aaron, Joshua, David, and Samson—not to mention the miracle-working prophet Elijah and those Jewish wonder women Ruth and Esther just to name a few. They all wielded courage and supernatural powers to protect and serve their people.

Within the cycle of the Jewish year, on holy days their amazing stories are retold: stories of hope and faith, guilt and redemption, atrocity and justice—of good prevailing over evil. These accounts are filled with more drama than anything Hollywood could ever imagine.

The sages expound that all human knowledge and wisdom is contained within the Bible's 304,805 letters in ink on parchment. (No wonder Jews are called the People of the Book!) The great eighteenth-century Hasidic master Rabbi Shneur Zalman of Liadi taught that Jews should relate the weekly Torah (Bible) portion to events in their own lives, right then and there. He called this way of reading "living with the times." As Eastern European Jewish immigrants poured into New York's Lower East Side in the 1900s, they too viewed the stories of the Bible through the prism of their hard lives in a sometimes baffling new land and passed them on to their children. And those children in turn retold those Jewish tales using dots of colored ink on pulp paper, beginning in the 1930s. (Actually, Superman was first drawn on cheap brown wrapping paper, but more on that later.)

In those days, the shadow of persecution was descending upon European Jews once more, and no one seemed willing to come to their rescue. The world needed heroes. So even before their own country went to battle with Hitler, young Jewish American artists and writers (some barely out of their teens) began creating powerful characters who were dedicated to protecting the innocent and conquering evil. By "living with the times" in their own outrageous way, this small band of Jewish men invented a whole new art form: the comic book.

Their names include Jerry Siegel and Joe Shuster, creators of Superman; Bob Kane (born Kahn) and Bill Finger, creators of Batman, and their protégé, Jerry Robinson, who invented the immortal villain the Joker; Will Eisner, creator of the Spirit and graphic novel pioneer; Julius Schwartz, the publisher known as the father of science fiction comics and the man behind the Justice League of America; Martin Nodell, the man behind the Green Lantern; Jack Kirby (born Jacob Kurtzberg) and Joe Simon, who brought the world Captain America; Max Gaines, the true father of comic books, his son William, publisher of *MAD* Magazine, and William's partner in satire, Harvey Kurtzman; Stan Lee (born Stanley Martin Lieber), who created Spider-Man, the Incredible Hulk, the Fantastic Four, and the X-Men; and Lee's boss, Martin Goodman of Marvel Comics.

The period after the end of World War II and the defeat of Adolf Hitler saw a brief decline in the popularity of superhero comics, but that didn't last long. Every generation needs archetypal heroes of its own, larger-than-life characters who evoke (sometimes blatantly, sometimes subconsciously) the eternal themes found in the Bible.

Each of the superheroes chronicled in this book personifies a theme or themes that figure prominently in the Jewish tradition:

- Superman—integrity
- Batman and the Spirit—justice
- Captain America—patriotism
- Justice League—teamwork
- Fantastic Four—family values
- Hulk—anger
- Spider-Man—responsibility and redemption
- X-Men—anti-Semitism and reconciliation

Today's graphic novels, while not concerned with superheroes, also explore the human condition in general (and Jewish American identity in particular) through the eyes of their Job-like antiheroes. In time, other Jewish names joined those of the pioneers: Gil Kane (born Eli Katz), Bob Kanigher, Chris Claremont, Joann Sfar, Diane Noomin, Joe Kubert, Harvey Pekar, and Art Spiegelman, to name a few.

Comics have evolved from "throwaway" escapism for children to a multimillion-dollar business encompassing print, movies, television, and toys. Comic books that our mothers once tossed out as trash are now worth thousands of dollars and studied within the highest levels of academia. Actor Nicholas Cage sold his extensive comic collection in 2002 for $1.68 million. (Incidentally, Cage took his stage name from a comic book character and named his son Kal-El, Superman's original, Kryptonian name.)[1] Also in 2002, the New York City Comic Book Museum released *C.O.M.I.C.S.* (Challenging Objective Minds: an Instructional Comic book Series), a curriculum for K–12 students used in dozens of schools.[2] The Library of Congress Comic Book Collection boasts over two thousand items, while the University of California, Riverside, the University of Missouri, and Michigan State University are just three American colleges boasting extensive comic book collections.[3]

Each generation of Jewish comic book creators explored the ambiguities of assimilation, the pain of discrimination, and the particularly Jewish theme of the misunderstood outcast, the rootless wanderer. Again and again, the triumph of good over evil remained a central comic book theme. Jack Kirby—known as the King of Comics—once said, "In the movies, the good always triumphed over evil. Underneath all the sophistication of modern comics, all the twists and psychological drama, good triumphs over evil. Those are the things I learned from my parents and from the Bible. It's part of my Jewish heritage."[4]

This book seeks to reclaim a vital component of that heritage. While the Jewish contribution to film, theater, music, and comedy is well known, the Jewish role in the creation of all-American superheroes is not—until now!

What spiritual guidance can be gleaned from these superheroes? The question is not as crazy as it sounds. This book teases out the biblical archetypes embodied in famous comic book characters, from the spider that saved King David to Moses's rescue from the bullrushes. It's a history lesson, Torah (Bible) study session, and survey of pop culture all in one.

We'll never know for sure how many thirteen-year-old boys squirreled themselves away with a stash of comic books when they were supposed to be studying for their bar mitzvahs. The thing is, they might have been on to something.

So let's start at the beginning. Up, up, and—oy vey!

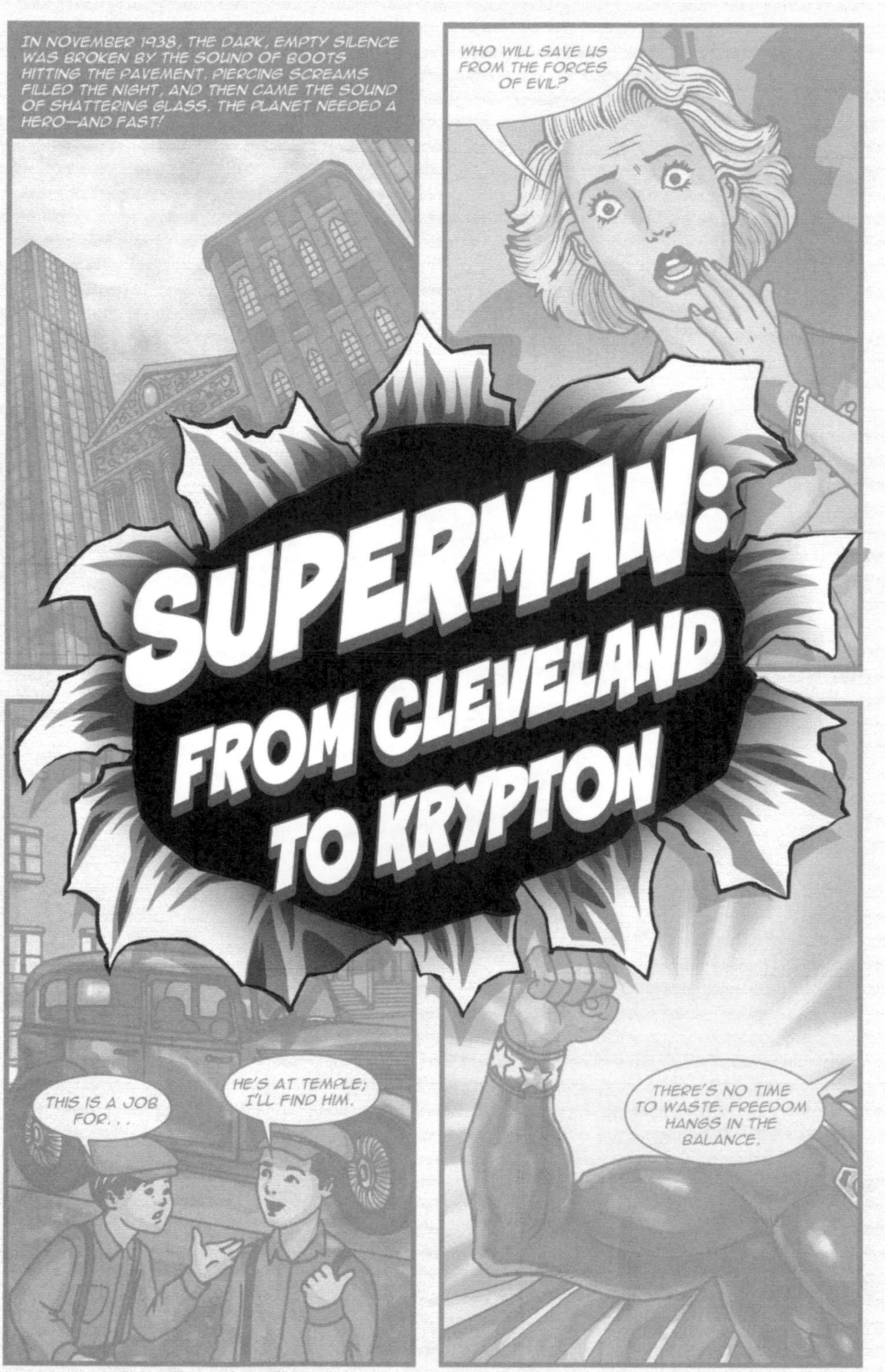
IN NOVEMBER 1938, THE DARK, EMPTY SILENCE WAS BROKEN BY THE SOUND OF BOOTS HITTING THE PAVEMENT. PIERCING SCREAMS FILLED THE NIGHT, AND THEN CAME THE SOUND OF SHATTERING GLASS. THE PLANET NEEDED A HERO—AND FAST!
WHO WILL SAVE US FROM THE FORCES OF EVIL?
SUPERMAN: FROM CLEVELAND TO KRYPTON
THIS IS A JOB FOR. . .
HE'S AT TEMPLE; I'LL FIND HIM.
THERE'S NO TIME TO WASTE. FREEDOM HANGS IN THE BALANCE.

SUPERHEROES

SUPERMAN

YEAR OF BIRTH: 1938

ALTER EGO: Kal-El (alien name), Clark Kent (human name)

OCCUPATION: Reporter

FIRST APPEARANCE IN A COMIC BOOK: *Action Comics* #1 (June 1938)

SUPERPOWERS: Enhanced strength and speed, invulnerability, special vision powers (x-ray, microscopic, heat)

ORIGIN OF SUPERPOWER: Solar rays

ARCHENEMY: Lex Luthor

BASE OF OPERATIONS: Metropolis

MEMBERSHIP: Justice League of America

CREATED BY: Jerry Siegel and Joe Shuster

FIRST DRAWN BY: Joe Shuster

JEWISH CONNECTION:

★ The recent *Action Comics* #835 (March 2006) introduced a character named Josef, a *kippah*-wearing Jewish reporter for the *Daily Planet*, who invites Superman to his home for a traditional Sabbath dinner. Josef makes a blessing on grape juice instead of wine because Superman does not drink alcohol. Superman particularly enjoys Josef's wife's kugel.

★ In the story "Miracle Monday" (*Superman* #400, 1984), citizens of sixtieth-century Earth celebrate their freedom with the "Miracle Monday dinner," commemorating the legend of Superman. Clear parallels are drawn between the Miracle Monday dinner and the Passover Seder, right down to the empty place setting and the phrases used during the celebration (for example, "Let all who are hungry come and eat! Let all who are in want come and—")

COMING OVER FROM THE OLD COUNTRY, CHANGING HIS NAME LIKE THAT. CLARK KENT, ONLY A JEW WOULD PICK A NAME LIKE THAT FOR HIMSELF.

—Michael Chabon, author, *The Amazing Adventures of Kavalier and Clay*

In November 1938, the dark, empty silence was broken by the sound of boots hitting pavement, then shouting, then shattering glass. In a matter of hours, Nazi storm troopers killed nearly one hundred German Jews, injured hundreds more, and burned 177 synagogues. The smashed windows of over seven thousand Jewish stores littered the streets. Soon the whole world would be engulfed in the blind hatred unleashed on this night, called Kristallnacht, "the Night of Broken Glass."

The planet needed a hero—fast. Who could have predicted that this hero would be one concocted by two Jewish boys in Ohio?

Jerry Siegel and Joe Shuster lived a mere twelve blocks apart in Cleveland. The pair collaborated on stories for their high school newspaper and shared a passion for science fiction and cheap pulp comics. In the 1930s, comic book publishing was still in its infancy. Like many young Jews with artistic aspirations, Siegel and Shuster yearned to break into this fledgling industry. It actively hired Jews, who were largely excluded from more "legitimate" illustration work. As *MAD* cartoonist Al Jaffee commented, "We couldn't get into newspaper strips or advertising; ad agencies wouldn't hire a Jew . . . [but] comic book publishers were Jewish."[1]

After all, anti-Semitism was a sad part of American life, too. In fact, the 1930s and 1940s were arguably the most anti-Semitic period in American history. Nazi sympathizer Fritz Kuhn of the German-American Bund led legions of rabid followers on marches through many cities, including Siegel and Shuster's hometown. Ivy League colleges kept the number of Jewish students to a minimum, while country clubs and even entire neighborhoods barred Jews altogether.

So Siegel and Shuster began submitting comic book treatments under the none-too-Jewish pseudonym Bernard J. Kenton, just to be on the safe side. Throughout the Great Depression, the two boys scraped together every penny they could just to cover postage, and Shuster sketched on cheap brown wrapping paper. Rejection letters followed, but the boys refused to accept defeat.

Eventually, they carved out a character that embodied their adolescent frustrations, served as a mouthpiece for the oppressed, and became an American icon.

Many years later, Jerry Siegel recalled the birth of Superman:

Late one night, it was so hot that I had trouble falling asleep. I passed the time by trying to come up with dramatic story elements for the comic strip. One premise I had already conceived came back to me, but in even sharper focus.

The story would begin with you as a child on far-off planet Krypton. Like the others of that world, you had super-powers. The child's scientist-father was mocked and denounced by the Science Council. They did not believe his claim that Krypton would soon explode from internal stresses. Convinced that his prediction was valid, the boy's father had been constructing a model rocket ship. As the planet began to perish, the baby's parents knew its end was close. There was not space enough for three people in the small model craft. They put the baby into it. The mother chose to remain on the doomed planet with the man she loved, and die with him. Tearfully, hoping that their baby boy would survive, they launched the craft toward the planet Earth. Shortly, Krypton exploded and its millions of inhabitants were destroyed.[2]

That was 1934, and it would take another four years for Superman to go from feverish dream to full-fledged hero. Detective Comics, Inc., looking for a character for its new magazine, *Action Comics*, paid young Siegel and Shuster $130 for the first thirteen pages of Superman. *Action Comics* #1 materialized in June 1938. The issue sold out, and a star was drawn. (One hopes the duo kept a few. Today, a mint copy of the issue is worth upwards of $450,000.)

In a brilliant stroke, Shuster and Siegel gave their superhuman hero a secret identity, that of an all-too-human reporter named Clark Kent. Practically speaking, this notion of a double identity allowed for almost endless storyline twists and thematic depth. On another level, it added considerably to the mythology that would eventually accrue around this fictional crime-fighter. From then on, double identities became a recurring theme throughout comic book culture and mythology, with *Spider-Man* and *Batman* employing this character device to great effect.

The Yiddish vernacular has many words to describe fellows like the shy, bumbling Clark: *nudge, schlepper, schmendrik,* and *schlimazel.* In the comic, Clark is simply called a klutz. Clark's shyness undermines his courtship of coworker Lois Lane. In *Action Comics* #1, a nervous Clark stammers, "W-what do you say to a-er-date tonight, Lois?"[3]—setting the tone of their relationship for years to come.

Siegel and Shuster admitted that the shy Clark struggling for a date reflected their own desire to gain social acceptance. Siegel recalled, "Much of that premise came out of my own personal frustrations. I wore spectacles and was a high school boy who wrote for the school newspaper . . . There were some lovely girls who I admired from afar . . . If I wore a colorful, skin-tight costume! If I could run faster than a train, lift great weights easily, and leap over skyscrapers in a single bound! Then they would notice me!"[4] Once Shuster earned enough money to pay the dues at a Cleveland health club, he spent hours trying to remold his body to more closely resemble that of his musclebound alter ego.

Of course, Superman's dual identity symbolizes something far deeper and more universal than the romantic yearnings of two particular young men. In his essay "Did You Know Superman Is Jewish?" Harry Brod elaborates: "The psychic trick Siegel and Shuster needed to pull off only worked if at the same time that we knew who Superman really was, we also knew that the world, in its stupidity, saw him only as Clark . . . the classic Jewish nebbish. But little did they know! Jewish men had only to tear off their clothes and throw off their glasses to reveal the surging superman underneath, physique fully revealed by those skin-tight red and blue tights, and flaunt that billowing cape."[5]

Consciously or not, Siegel and Shuster tapped into a renewed sense of American patriotism with impeccable timing. *Superman* #1 was published in the summer of 1939, more than two years before America entered World War II. In the issue, Clark and Lois travel to a thinly disguised Nazi Germany, where Lois ends up in front of a firing squad. She's rescued by Superman, naturally.

In the real Germany of 1939, Adolf Hitler was exploiting his nation's economic and social ills by scapegoating Jews. First, gold and silver owned by Jewish citizens was confiscated. Then, German Jews were forbidden to hold government jobs, go out at night, or even own radios. Some who tried to escape on the S.S. *St. Louis* were denied sanctuary in the United States and sent back to Europe. Living in a country that had stripped them of their citizenship yet perversely obstructed their exit, German Jews resorted to desperate measures. Just as the baby Superman was sent away from Krypton to avoid the mass destruction of his people, many Jewish children were sent on the Kindertransports to seek safety with families in England.

Ironically, Hitler's "master race" ideology is often mistakenly associated with philosopher Friedrich Nietzsche's concept of the *ubermensch*, or "superman." Nietzsche believed that religion and traditional values made men weak. Only by overcoming such influences and determining values of his own, said Nietzsche, could man realize his full potential. After his death, his views were increasingly linked directly to Nazi philosophy.

In *Superman* #10 (1941), Clark and Lois are dispatched to cover the Dukalia American Sports Festival, which looks remarkably like the infamous 1936 Berlin Olympics, which Hitler had mistakenly believed would demonstrate German superiority to the whole world, once and for all. The Dukalian athletes march around the stadium, arms stretched in a "Heil Hitler" pose, and Dukalian consul Karl Wolf, who personifies Hitler, bellows to the crowd: "Present here is the flower of the Dukalian youth! You have seen them perform physical feats which no other human beings can. Proof, I tell you, that we Dukalians are superior to any other race or nation! Proof that we are entitled to be the masters of America!"[6] Clark soon enters the games as Superman and humiliates the fascist Dukalians. This dark-haired heir of Moses defeats the Aryans on their own field. Superman, the literary child of Jews, became on pulp paper what Hitler could not create even on the ashes of millions of flesh-and-blood Jewish children: the *ubermensch*.

News of Superman and his ethnic undertones did not escape the enemy's notice in real life. Josef Goebbels, the Nazi minister of propaganda, denounced Superman as a Jew. In April 1940, *Das Schwarze Korps*, the weekly newspaper of the Nazi SS, attacked the comic and its Jewish writers: "Jerry Siegel, an intellectually and physically circumcised chap who has his headquarters in New York . . . The inventive Israelite named this pleasant guy with an overdeveloped body and underdeveloped mind 'Superman' . . . As you can see, there is nothing the Sadducees won't do for money! . . . Jerry Siegellack stinks. Woe to the American youth, who must live in such a poisoned atmosphere and don't even notice the poison they swallow daily."[7]

Here were would-be world conquerors wringing their hands over a cartoon character cooked up by a couple of boys across the sea. Yet this hysterical, ideologically driven rant actually touched on something vital: the importance of Shuster and Siegel's Jewish heritage.

While a number of influences have been cited for their Superman creation—the movies of Douglas Fairbanks, the science fiction of Edgar Rice Burroughs, Greek mythology, Arthurian legend, Western folk heroes, and American cartoon icons such as Popeye—Shuster and Siegel's Jewish heritage was perhaps their greatest inspiration. *Superman* #1 begins with a brief synopsis of Superman's escape from Krypton, which draws heavily on Jewish geographical, historical, and biblical sources.

For example, Superman's journey closely reflects the story of Moses. Like the people of Krypton who faced annihilation, the Jews of biblical Egypt faced the murder of all their male offspring. To ensure her son's survival, Jochebed places Moses in a reed basket and sets him afloat on the Nile. Her desperate decision is clearly echoed by Superman's father, Jor-El, who launches the little rocket ship containing his son into outer space.

Moses and Superman are eventually discovered and raised in foreign cultures. Baby Moses is found by Basya, the daughter of Pharaoh, and raised in the royal palace. Superman is found by Jonathan and Martha Kent in a midwestern cornfield and given the name Clark. From the onset, both Basya and the Kents realize that these foundling boys are extraordinary.

When Clark grows older, his adoptive father tells him, "Now listen to me, Clark, this great strength of yours—you've got to hide it from people or they'll be scared of you . . . but when the proper time comes you must use it to assist humanity."[8] Moses gets a similar inspirational talk from God in the famous story of the burning bush from the book of Exodus: "And now, go and I shall dispatch you to Pharaoh and you shall take my people the children of Israel out of Egypt."[9]

Superman leads a double life as the stuttering, spectacle-wearing reporter whose true identity no one suspects. In the same way, for his own safety, Moses kept his Jewish roots hidden for a time. Furthermore, because he had a stammer, Moses sometimes needed his brother Aaron to speak for him.

Superman's original name on Krypton also reveals biblical underpinnings. Superman is named Kal-El and his father Jor-El. The suffix "El" is one of the ancient names for God used throughout the Bible. It is also found in the names of great prophets, such as Isra-el, Samu-el, and Dani-el and angels, such as Micha-el and Gavri-el. According to Jewish tradition, Micha-el is the great combatant angel who fights Satan. He could easily be deemed the flying Superman's biblical alter ego. The prefix of Superman's name, "Kal," is the root of several Hebrew words meaning "with lightness," "swiftness," "vessel" and "voice." We may never know whether Siegel and Shuster were aware of these precise Hebrew translations; nevertheless, the character's name could not be more apt.

Throughout the early comics, the biblical influence on the Superman story is clear. *Action Comics* #7 (1938) opens with the statement "Friend of the helpless and oppressed is Superman, a man possessing the strength of a dozen Samsons!"[10]

In the Bible story, Samson possesses extraordinary physical strength. He falls victim to his enemies, the Philistines, after Delilah makes him reveal the secret of his strength: his long hair. Delilah cuts Samson's hair, weakening him. In a final act of courage, Samson calls out, "Lord God! Remember me and strengthen me just this one time."[11] Samson proceeds to smash the pillars supporting the building, and the temple falls on the Philistine chiefs. Like Samson, Superman has a weakness: exposure to the mysterious mineral kryptonite saps his strength.

In *Superman* #2 (1939), Clark interviews scientist Adolphus Runyan. Runyan has discovered a gas so powerful "it is capable of penetrating any type of gas-mask."[12] Adolphus Runyan was in fact a thinly disguised caricature of Adolf Hitler, who really used poison gas. In the comic book, the gas falls into enemy hands and Superman travels to an unnamed war zone to fight. When he finds himself in an ancient pillared room, Superman smashes the pillars supporting the walls and shouts, "A guy named Samson once had this idea!"[13]

Ethics of the Fathers, a famous Tractate (section) in the Mishnah (which codifies the Jewish oral tradition) deals with morality; many of its vignettes easily apply to the Superman ethos. For example, one section of *Ethics* tells us that "the world endures on three things: justice, truth, and peace."[14] In the same way, Superman stands for three things: "Truth, justice, and the American way." Another part of *Ethics* declares that one should strive to "be bold as a leopard, light as an eagle, swift as a deer, and strong as a lion."[15] Superman embodies similarly powerful, if more modern, attributes. He is "faster than a speeding bullet, more powerful than a locomotive, and able to leap tall buildings in a single bound."

The sixteenth-century kabbalist Rabbi Isaac Luria, known as the Arizal, taught that the world was created through the remnants of divine sparks and the vessels intended to hold them. Due to a cosmic catastrophe, these vessels could not contain the sparks, so they shattered. This is known as *shevirat ha-Kelim* ("breaking of the vessels"). Our world is composed of the shards of these broken vessels. The job of mankind is to reunite the shards with their divine source, a process called *tikkun haolam* ("repairing the world"). The destruction of Krypton can be seen as the breaking of these primordial vessels, giving birth to Superman, who, like all of us, is called to restore order and balance in the world. We may not do it while wearing a cape and a big *S* on our chests, but the universal message still comes across clearly via the unlikely vehicle of a comic book for children. It's as if Siegel and Shuster had subconsciously tapped into Kabbalah, the very core of Jewish spirituality!

Superman's unexpected depths made this symbol of all things American a muse of sorts to artists—musicians in particular. In the 1960s and 1970s, the character's name evoked cheerful, whimsical optimism in songs like Donovan's "Sunshine Superman" (1965). As time went on, postmodern cynicism took hold, and Superman became a symbol of irony and disillusionment. Compositions such as "O Superman" by Laurie Anderson (1981), "Superman's Song" by the Crash Test Dummies (1991), and "Superman (It's Not Easy)" by Five for Fighting (2000) are melancholy dirges. Superman hasn't come to our rescue. He's only human after all, and, in the case of "Superman's Song," dead and buried.

From the very start, Superman also inspired creations of a slightly less elevated nature. *Action Comics* #1 led to *Superman* #1—a comic all his own. A radio series, animated series, and movie serial followed, then a hugely popular television show starring George Reeves. The Man of Steel even spawned a 1966 Broadway musical called *It's a Bird . . . It's a Plane . . . It's Superman*. Then came the 1978 blockbuster movie *Superman*, starring the late Christopher Reeve, who embodied the character so perfectly that the actor's quadriplegia later in life was a poignant irony.

But not even the Presbyterian Reeve was able to eliminate the persistent connection between Superman and Jewish culture. During the 1990s, Superman had a whimsical recurring role on the small screen's longest running tribute to New York Jewishness: as a magnet on Jerry's refrigerator in the hit show *Seinfeld*. Jerry's constant references to the superhero even led to a number of memorable American Express commercials, depicting Seinfeld and an animated Superman as great friends.

Across the pond, the BBC's Radio 4 ran a debate in 2005 called "Is Superman Jewish?" leading to this comment by Howard Jacobson for the *Times* (London): "Touch Superman with kryptonite and he is no longer his adopted self, no longer Clark Kent, but Kal-El, the boy with the kabbalistic name, the boy from the shtetl. Superman might be Jewish, but it's only so long as no one knows he's Jewish that he is capable of performing wonders. And you can't get more Jewish than that."[16]

Created by two sons of Jewish immigrants, Superman—the extraterrestrial alien turned all-American icon—is a powerful symbol of assimilation. Harvard professor Henry Lewis Gates Jr. called Superman "the hero from Ellis Island" who personified the "undocumented alien who had been naturalized by the ultimate American couple."[17] Interpreting the character's symbolic meaning, cartoonist and screenwriter Jules Feiffer points to the "old country" so many Jewish immigrants to America left behind: "It wasn't Krypton that Superman came from; it was the planet Minsk or Lodz or Vilna or Warsaw."[18]

In April 1998, DC Comics released an ambitious three-part Superman story (#80–#82) to celebrate a monumental milestone: the sixtieth anniversary of Superman's debut in *Action Comics* #1. This new story's postmodern "what if" scenario explored the Man of Steel's Semitic origins in a way that would have been unthinkable back in 1938.

The opening panels of issue #80 mirror those of the original *Action Comics* #1 almost exactly, with Superman coming to the rescue in a series of fairly pedestrian dilemmas. Then the plot takes a turn. The very real Nazi threat that had been left unspoken by Siegel and Shuster in the original 1938 comic is now brought into full focus.

In downtown Metropolis—Superman's very own turf—a rally of Nazi sympathizers has drawn an enormous crowd. A blond-haired, blue-eyed Hollywood star, famous for his role as an onscreen superhero, declares himself the personification of the Nazi "superman": "The ideal of the pure Aryan *ubermensch* who will lead the master race to a new heroic age is more than a dream! I stand before you as proof!"

But the actor is helpless when the cable supporting the massive swastika hanging above his podium suddenly snaps and the sign crashes toward the earth, threatening hundreds of lives. Superman swoops down and pushes the giant sign away with seconds to spare. Then, to his horror, he hears the fascist actor praising him—Superman—as a true hero, the real *ubermensch*!

Appalled, the Man of Steel takes the microphone: "Listen up folks. Call me what you want, but I will never be a champion of Nazism! I will not be anyone's symbol of hate, racial prejudice and genocide! I am an American like all true Americans; I must strive to be a champion of tolerance and diversity . . . justice and kindness!"[19]

In #81, reporter Clark Kent is sent on assignment "to get the real scoop on the Nazi occupation of Poland." So Superman dons a disguise of a different kind—the humble garb of a *shtetl* (the Yiddish term for a heavily Jewish populated small town in pre-Holocaust Central and Eastern Europe) resident. In Poland, he witnesses Nazi brutality firsthand but worries that turning into Superman to stop it might make matters worse. So Clark is forced to join the suffering Jews. He befriends two young boys named Moishe and Baruch and assists them in a task more harrowing than anything Superman has ever faced—they are forced to fill a mass grave with the bodies of the Nazis' victims.

Moishe and Baruch welcome Clark to their home, where Baruch begins doodling on a scrap of brown paper. Moishe explains, "Baruch's drawing our angel again! I make up the stories and he makes up the pictures." The boy's grandfather adds, "He sounds like more of a golem than an angel." The grandfather notices Clark's puzzled expression. "Your *bubeh* never told you stories of golems!!? The golem was a statue that came to life when the written name of God was put in its mouth. He would become a fearsome mighty creature that would drive away enemies and save the people!"[20]

It's a poignant touch. Moishe and Baruch are clearly intended to remind readers of Siegel and Shuster, whose key role in the history of comic books was at last being recognized. At the time this issue appeared, Michael Chabon was working on the novel that would become *The Amazing Adventures of Kavalier and Clay*, which went on to win a Pulitzer Prize in 2001. That sprawling tale of golems and superheroes was inspired by a magazine article Chabon had read about the strange fate of Siegel and Shuster, who, having sold the rights to Superman for $130, lost control of their world-famous creation until a campaign by legions of fans in the 1970s finally earned them the recognition they'd deserved. Kavalier and Clay's endearing story introduced millions to the Jewish–comic book connection and helped to further legitimize comics as a literary art form.

In the final installment of the anniversary story, Superman rescues Lois Lane from a crowded cattle car just before it reaches the Treblinka concentration camp. Then he joins the Jewish resistance, fighting along-side real-life hero Mordecai Anielewicz. Anielwicz ignited the single larg-est Jewish armed resistance against the Nazis: the Warsaw Ghetto Upris-ing. While heavily outnumbered, members of the resistance held off the Germans for more than sixty days until their opponents burned down the ghetto block by block. Just before his death, Anielewicz wrote to a friend: "Jewish self-defense in the ghetto has been realized. Jewish retaliation and resistance has become a fact. I have been witness to the magnificent heroic battle of the Jewish fighters."[21]

At the very end of the story, Superman defeats the Nazis and smashes through the cement wall of the Warsaw Ghetto—beyond which lies Metropolis, circa 1998! Confused, Superman muses to Lois, "It's like we've had a whole other life together. I can remember a whole childhood in the 1920's." Which of course, in a sense, he did—a childhood lived by his two young Jewish creators in Cleveland, Ohio.

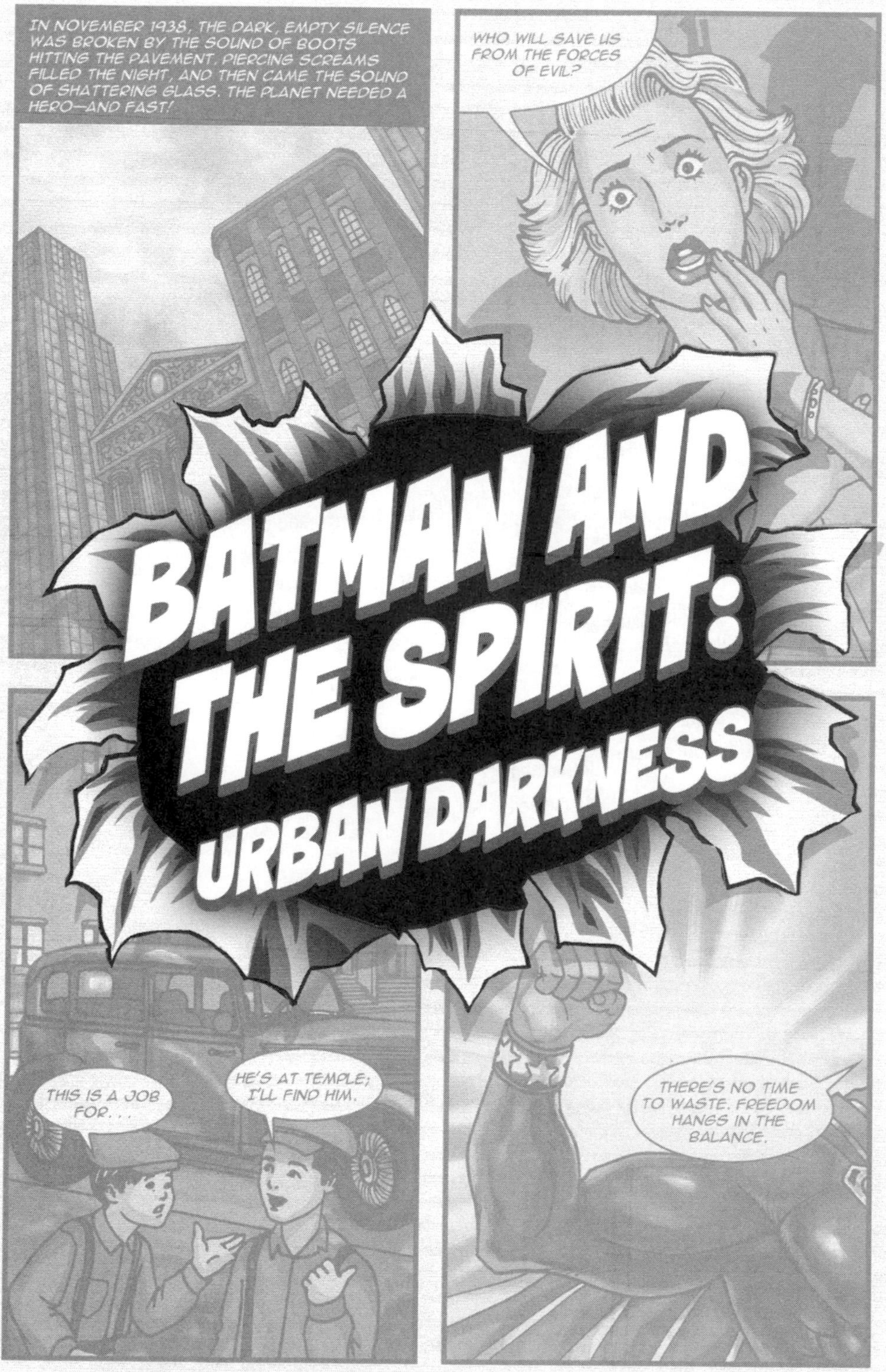

IN NOVEMBER 1938, THE DARK, EMPTY SILENCE WAS BROKEN BY THE SOUND OF BOOTS HITTING THE PAVEMENT. PIERCING SCREAMS FILLED THE NIGHT, AND THEN CAME THE SOUND OF SHATTERING GLASS. THE PLANET NEEDED A HERO—AND FAST!
WHO WILL SAVE US FROM THE FORCES OF EVIL?
BATMAN AND THE SPIRIT: URBAN DARKNESS
THIS IS A JOB FOR . . .
HE'S AT TEMPLE; I'LL FIND HIM.
THERE'S NO TIME TO WASTE. FREEDOM HANGS IN THE BALANCE.

BATMAN

YEAR OF BIRTH: 1939

ALTER EGO: Bruce Wayne

OCCUPATION: High-society millionaire, industrialist, and philanthropist

FIRST APPEARANCE IN A COMIC BOOK: *Detective Comics* #27 (May 1939)

SUPERPOWERS: None; relies on his Olympic-level strength, speed, and agility and an array of gadgets, such as his state-of-the-art vehicles and the tools in his utility belt.

ORIGIN OF SUPERPOWER: Training of his body and mind to the height of perfection over many years

ARCHENEMY: The Joker

BASE OF OPERATIONS: Gotham City

MEMBERSHIP: Justice League of America

CREATED BY: Bob Kane and Jerry Robinson

FIRST DRAWN BY: Bob Kane

JEWISH CONNECTION:

In the imaginary Elseworlds story "Berlin Batman" (*Batman Chronicles* #11, winter 1998), Batman's alter ego is Jewish artist Baruch Wane, who is a friend of Komissar Gordon (a Nazi).

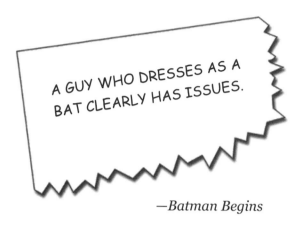

A GUY WHO DRESSES AS A BAT CLEARLY HAS ISSUES.

—Batman Begins

Siegel and Shuster were not the only young Jewish artists setting out to save the world. Growing up in the Bronx in the Depression were two young Jewish bruisers who first crossed paths at De Witt Clinton High School. In his autobiography, *Batman and Me*, Bob Kahn (who later changed his name to Kane) recalled his major competitor for cartoon space in the school newspaper, the *Clinton News*. "Another young artist was competing with me to be top cartoonist on the *News*. Unfortunately, my competitor got more of his cartoons into print than I did, and I must admit that he was a better artist than I was. His name was Will Eisner."[1]

Also attending De Witt around this time were Bill Finger (class of 1932), Stanley Lieber (class of 1939), and Irwin Hansen (class of 1939). All went on to take part in the Jewish transformation of American entertainment in general and comics in particular.

Kane and Eisner were second-generation Americans, two among the millions who experienced hardship during the Great Depression. Kane recalled, "These were the days of massive unemployment and widespread poverty, when people who had once worked for a living and been proudly independent were forced to stand idly in bread lines waiting for a hand-out."[2] Between 1929 and 1939, the stock market crashed, thousands of banks failed, and U.S. unemployment soared to 25 percent. Did witnessing this devastation inspire the young Kane and Eisner to try, somehow, to mend society's ills?

Like the creators of Superman, art school graduates Eisner and Kane gravitated toward comic illustration. It was one of the only publishing enterprises then open to hiring Jews, at a time when jobs of any kind were hard to come by. Each of these two young men created an enduring superhero—Kane with Batman and Eisner with the Spirit. Both super-heroes, like their authors, were Bronx-born fighters fated to fend for themselves.

In the wake of Superman's spectacular success, National Periodical Publications editor Vin Sullivan asked Kane to develop a new character. Kane immediately contacted fellow De Witt graduate Bill Finger. Together, this De Witt dynamic duo forged a strange yet oddly appealing character: millionaire playboy Bruce Wayne, who fights criminals while wearing a bat costume. Batman debuted in *Detective Comics #27* (May 1939). As Salon.com's Bob Callahan noted on the occasion of Kane's death, "Superman had captured the market for the all-American type. But there was still room—hell, there may always be room—for a man with a weird idea about a bat."[3]

Kane later recalled his tough childhood in the East Bronx, where the streets "were melting pots composed of different ethnic groups and often one nationality would be pitted against another. In order to survive, if one were a loner like myself, he would have to join his neighborhood gang for protection."[4] Bruce Wayne is a loner, too, who through sheer hard work becomes a master thinker as well as a fighter. And Kane ensured that his creation got to play with the kinds of toys his younger self could only have dreamed of.

In the first issues, Batman was simply a one-dimensional vigilante in a weird outfit, devoid of motivation or much personality. Even his location was obscure. Long after Batman had reached iconic status, co-creator Finger claimed he'd simply filched the name "Gotham City" from a phone book listing for "Gotham Jewelers." Yet the peculiar name for Batman's New York–inspired stomping grounds evokes, intentionally or not, the word "gothic"—an apt adjective for the eerie indigo streets and looming towers depicted as the superhero's home.

Writing about Batman, comic book historian and creator Alan Oirich observed, "In the late 1930s, Jews in some of the capitals of Europe were being killed in the streets, with high culture and gothic architecture serving as settings for acts of uncivilized violence . . . Like the aghast eight year old [Bruce Wayne], post-Holocaust Jews have witnessed the generation before them shot down in the streets. They struggle to understand, to avenge and to decide what in the world to do in response to such unfathomable tragedy."[5]

Oirich was referring to the story of Bruce Wayne's parents. In November 1939, *Batman* readers finally learned what was driving this mysterious "caped crusader": While walking home from the theater, the parents of young Bruce Wayne had been murdered before his eyes by a petty thief attempting to steal his mother's necklace. Bruce vowed to avenge his parents' deaths by spending the rest of his life fighting criminals. His generous inheritance gives him the resources he requires to become a "master scientist" and to mold his physique "until he is able to perform amazing athletic feats."[6] Finally, a now grown up Bruce contemplates a disguise for his crime-fighting escapades. When a bat flies into his study, Bruce Wayne's backstory is complete. Batman, another orphaned superhero, is born.

To temper Batman's darkness, the comic needed a more kid-friendly tone. Kane decided a sidekick would be a useful storytelling device, and so Robin the Boy Wonder joined the *Batman* cast. The very first issue depicting Batman's new partner sold double the usual run.

Partnerships like this one are prominent in the Jewish religion. The book of Ecclesiastes sums up the advantage of two individuals working steadfastly together: "Two are better than one, for they get a greater reward for their labor. For should they fall, one can lift the other; but woe to him who is alone when he falls and there is no one to lift him!"[7]

One by one, Batman's foes made their debuts as well: Catwoman, Two-Face, the Penguin, the Riddler, and, most famously, the Joker. Fans owe the Joker's existence to a chance encounter in the famed "borscht belt," a popular resort area and proving ground for the nation's Jewish stand-up comedians. "In late 1939, I was taking a respite from my drawing board during the summer at a hotel in the Catskill mountains (probably Grossingers), when I met seventeen-year-old Jerry Robinson,"[8] Kane wrote. The Jewish journalism student—and future creator of the Joker—was innocently pacing the tennis court when Kane noticed the young man's impressive hand-painted jacket and offered him a chance to join his artistic team. "I have often wondered what I'd be doing if I hadn't been there on the tennis court that day,"[9] Robinson later commented.

During World War II, Batman sat out the battle overseas and focused on wrongdoing on the home front. Perhaps not coincidentally, Kane and Finger were classified as 4-F, excluded from the military for health reasons. In an issue entitled "Swastika over the White House" (*Batman* #14, 1943), Batman and Robin defeat a Nazi mob in America, capturing it in its own giant swastika.

Kane once disclosed that Batman was the embodiment of his own dreams: "My wish fulfillment self is really Bruce Wayne, the Batman. He is the epitome of every fantasy I ever had as a youngster . . . a rich philanthropist who would cloak his identity under a mask and crusade for justice in the guise of a superhero . . . I uphold the same principles for which Batman fights. I am a great believer in righteousness and abhor man's injustice towards his fellow man."[10]

Kane's exercise in personal wish fulfillment struck a chord with tens of millions of readers, and Batman became a mainstream success. A campy, cult classic on the small screen, *Batman* also inspired feature films of varying quality and popularity in the 1990s and into the twenty-first century.

One Batman film spawned a particularly bizarre controversy. In a 1992 *New York Times* op-ed, a pair of earnest Columbia University students denounced *Batman Returns* as—of all things—anti-Semitic. The Tim Burton movie, they wrote, contained "biblical allusions and historical references which betray a hidden conflict between gentile and Jew."

The two journalists leveled their strangest charge against Burton's vision of the Penguin, portrayed by actor Danny De Vito. This character, wrote Rebecca Roiphe and Daniel Cooper, "is a Jew, down to his hooked nose, pale face, and lust for herring."[11] For example, at the beginning of the film, a basket carries the baby Penguin through the sewers of Gotham City in a pastiche of the Moses story. (Of course, this is also a twisted nod to Superman's own Mosaic origins as the infant refugee from Krypton.)

Ben Macintyre dismissed the whole controversy in the *Times* (London): "Perhaps the most telling response to the fracas over Batman's alleged racism came from a young girl, whose father read her the article: 'It made me very surprised,' she wrote, 'when they said the Penguin had to be Jewish because of his nose and fondness for herring. For Pete's sake, he's a penguin, give him a break.'"[12]

One perennial feature in Batman lore is the superhero's famous hideout, the Batcave, which first appeared in *Batman* #48 (1948). That issue begins, "Deep under the surface of Gotham City is a mammoth cave which is known but to two people—Batman and Robin! For this is the Batman's subterranean retreat—The Batcave!"[13]

The notion of a cave representing a private place of introspection and spiritual growth is a biblical one. The book of Genesis recounts the purchase of the cave of Machpelah by Abraham as a burial plot for his wife, Sarah. *Machpelah* means "doubled" in Hebrew, which hints at the holy couples buried there: Adam and Eve, Abraham and Sarah, Isaac and Rebecca, and Jacob and Leah. This cave was also a place where warring brothers were able to unite—Isaac and Ishmael buried their father, Abraham, together; in turn, Jacob and Esau buried their father, Isaac.

In Talmudic times, Rabbi Shimon Bar Yochai and his son Elazar fled the Roman army and hid in a cave in the northern region of Israel. For the next thirteen years, father and son spent their entire days immersed in Torah study, honing their spiritual powers. It is believed that Rabbi Shimon wrote the Zohar, the primary work of Kabbalah, during this time of introspection. Like their comic book alter egos, Batman and Robin, they attempted to heal the world from a secret retreat.

Batman's fame and popularity endured and shows no sign of abating. "Some of us are blessed to write a few memorable poems; others may pen a fine first novel," wrote Bob Callahan in his Kane obituary in Salon.com. "But few of us luck into the creation of a bona fide American archetype."[14]

Even fewer artists actually invent a brand-new literary genre, and in Will Eisner's case, luck had nothing to do with it. Always a better artist and writer than Kane, Eisner started out as his high school classmate's boss. After college, Eisner set up an outfit with Jerry Iger, and they hired like-minded Jewish artists, such as Kane and Jack Kirby, none of whom had any previous comic book experience. In one spectacular early blunder, Eisner rejected Siegel and Shuster's *Superman* when it was submitted to him. "I sent it back to Cleveland," Eisner recalled later, "and told them they weren't ready."[15] In those days, he added, comic books were "regarded as 'trash and junk' and, like the rag and junk trades, the only people who would go into them were people who had very little opportunity anywhere else. Young Jewish artists quickly gravitated to comic books."

Eisner was eventually lured to Quality Comics, where he was instrumental in the creation of *Blackhawk* (with its team of multinational Nazi-fighting fliers) and the character Uncle Sam (perhaps the ultimate assimilation fantasy). While at Quality, Eisner wrote and drew a new title, *The Spirit*, which became a critical and commercial smash. Sometimes called the *Citizen Kane* of comics, *The Spirit* combined action and fun with a previously unseen maturity that appealed to children and adults alike.

The Spirit's Central City was yet another alternative New York. Like Batman, the Spirit is a vigilante crime-fighter with a hidden identity. After a run-in with a criminal leaves Denny Colt presumed dead, he assumes the life of a crime-fighter called the Spirit. And just as Batman has a close relationship with police commissioner Jim Gordon, the Spirit has a similar relationship with Eustace Dolan.

However, the Spirit was not cloaked in spandex but wore a snazzy, noir-inspired blue suit. His only disguise was a matching blue eye mask, a reluctant concession to Eisner's publishers, who insisted that every superhero needed one. "I tried every device I could think of to remove his mask, because it was getting in the way; I found his believability was being impaired,"[16] Eisner noted.

Perhaps this difference signifies a deeper chasm in Kane's and Eisner's acceptance of their own identities. Tellingly, Eisner, unlike Kane, never changed his name to make it sound less Jewish. On the other hand, Kane went to so much trouble to conceal his own Jewish identity that he didn't even mention it in his autobiography. In years to come, Eisner openly and seriously explored his Jewish identity through his work. "Although we may have thought we were creating Aryan characters, with non-Jewish names like Bruce Wayne, Clark Kent and my own Denny Colt," Eisner explained, "I think we were responding to an inner *neshama* that responds to forces around us—just like the story of the Golem in Jewish lore."[17]

Neshama is the Hebrew word for the "soul of a Jew," which according to mystical sources comes from the innermost essence of God—even if this connection is disguised by a gentile-sounding name. *Pintele Yid* is a Yiddish term meaning "the Jewish spark that patiently yearns to return to things of the spirit." The term is also synonymous with the simple, uneducated Jew who, while lacking in knowledge, is still a believer. Eisner once commented, "I'm part of a generation that was very conscious of our Jewishness, but we were not scholars. As time went on, I developed a strong Jewish identity. I read as much about Jewish things as I can. Right now, I'm working my way through Maimonides and through Paul Johnson's *History of the Jews*."[18]

The Spirit's possible Jewish identity has been the subject of much speculation. "His name might have been Denny Colt but he was clearly circumcised,"[19] Art Spiegelman noted. Another Pulitzer Prize–winning cartoonist, Jules Feiffer (who once worked on *The Spirit*), famously commented, "The Spirit reeked of lower middle class: his nose may have turned up, but we all knew he was Jewish."[20]

While Eisner did not intend for the Spirit to be an overtly Jewish character, he added, "Comics are to art what Yiddish is to language. It is the vernacular language of a certain kind, they embrace and subsume a lot of other things into its cholent [cultural mix] and makes this kind of weird stew."[21]

During the war, Eisner illustrated *Army Motors,* the army's monthly preventative maintenance magazine. Eventually, Eisner lost his will to write *The Spirit* and in 1952 became head of production of the military magazine *P*S,* where he remained for twenty years. His efforts appealed greatly to soldiers, whose attention spans and levels of literacy necessarily ranged widely. Through his irreverent, sometimes risqué, illustrations, Eisner taught a generation of military personnel to repair and preserve equipment. That is to say, Eisner saved real lives while the Spirit saved fictional ones.

In the 1970s, the always restless Eisner began experimenting in a new genre called the graphic novel, presenting serious, adult themes in comic book format—something he'd been groping toward since *The Spirit* and even his army safety manuals. (In the conclusion, we'll explore the graphic novel in greater detail.)

◆ • ◆

Although Batman and the Spirit had Jewish creators, attempts to attach biblical alter egos to them present serious difficulties at first. Those who break the law (even while trying to uphold it) and act violently are deemed vigilantes according to Jewish law, no better than the criminals they purport to fight. The book of Leviticus states, "You shall not take revenge and you shall not bear a grudge against the members of your people; you shall love your fellow as yourself."[22] It is troubling (and distinctly "un-Jewish") when any act of violence is celebrated and honored. Batman and the Spirit are not even imbued with supernatural powers. Shouldn't they let those already sworn to uphold the law do their jobs?

The book of Numbers tells the story of Aaron's grandson, a young, hot-blooded zealot named Pinchas. After witnessing gross immorality and pagan worship at the very foot of the Tabernacle of Holiness, Pinchas takes the law into his own hands. He picks up a spear and impales the culprits in full view of Moses, Aaron, and the leaders of Israel.

Pinchas acted violently, yet the Bible refers to him as a descendant of Aaron the priest and a great peacemaker of the Jewish people. The story of Pinchas (like that of his comic book alter egos Batman and the Spirit) teaches that sometimes the only way to restore peace and harmony is to confront injustice. Pinchas was praised for his actions. He was awarded the Covenant of Peace and appointed to the priesthood.

Another analogous story of vengeance is found in the life of Moses. Moses is walking through a field when he witnesses an Egyptian smiting a Jew. We are told that Moses "turned this way and that and saw that there was no man, so he struck down the Egyptian."[23]

Like Pinchas, the young Moses took the law into his own hands. Moses looked "this way and that" to see if anybody was a witness to his actions. However, another interpretation is that Moses looked not to see if people were watching him but to see if anybody else would protect the Jew being beaten. When no one else came to the rescue, Moses (like the fictional Batman and the Spirit) felt forced to act.

While Judaism does not condone vigilante justice, in the book of Exodus, God gives the Jewish people a perplexing instruction for implementing justice: "An eye for an eye, a tooth for a tooth, a hand for a hand, a foot for a foot, a burn for a burn, a wound for a wound, a bruise for a bruise."[24] While this seems like a mandate for vengeance and barbarism, the Talmud in Ketubot 32b and Baba Kamma 83b explains that "an eye for an eye" represents monetary compensation, an "eye's worth for an eye." The financial compensation should equal the amount of damage that has been inflicted—no more, no less. One is reminded of the words of Teviyah in *Fiddler on the Roof*: "If everyone lived by 'an eye for an eye and a tooth for a tooth,' the world would be blind and toothless." Teviyah might well be right. However, the Torah clearly states that evil must be met with punishment in order for justice to prevail.

If the world ignores injustice, individuals are obliged to keep peace. "Where there are no leaders, strive to be a leader,"[25] states *Ethics of the Fathers*. Batman and the Spirit demonstrated this philosophy. Perhaps donning a bat suit or the identity of a supernatural private eye is a little extreme, but the message is clear. Unlike Superman—whose masked self *was* his real identity—Bruce Wayne and Denny Colt were real people with real vulnerabilities, people whom readers can relate to and even admire. Whether readers (or even their own creators) realize it or not, these heroes personify particular Jewish traditions and values.

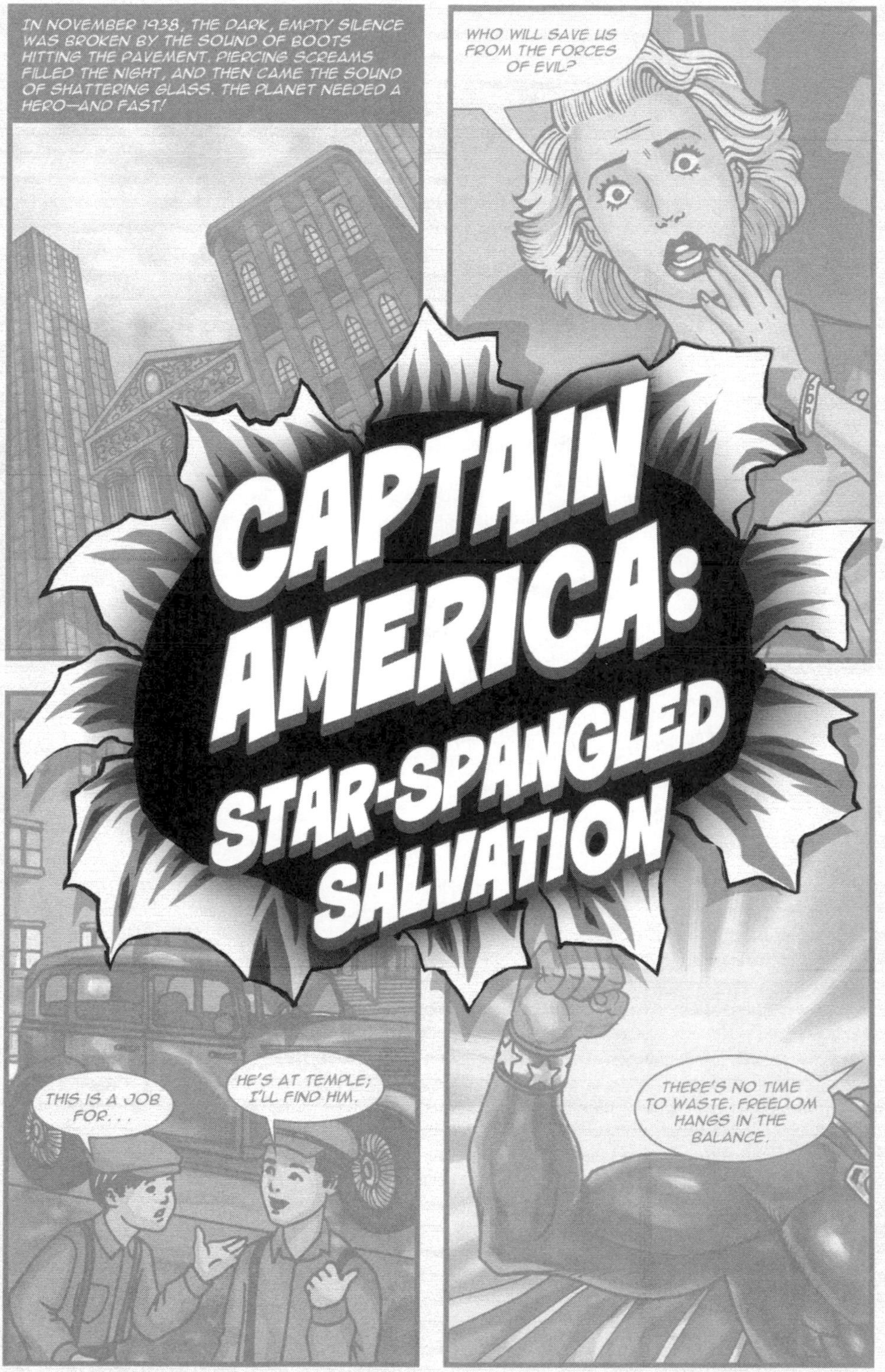
IN NOVEMBER 1938, THE DARK, EMPTY SILENCE WAS BROKEN BY THE SOUND OF BOOTS HITTING THE PAVEMENT. PIERCING SCREAMS FILLED THE NIGHT, AND THEN CAME THE SOUND OF SHATTERING GLASS. THE PLANET NEEDED A HERO—AND FAST!
WHO WILL SAVE US FROM THE FORCES OF EVIL?
CAPTAIN AMERICA: STAR-SPANGLED SALVATION
THIS IS A JOB FOR. . .
HE'S AT TEMPLE; I'LL FIND HIM.
THERE'S NO TIME TO WASTE. FREEDOM HANGS IN THE BALANCE.

CAPTAIN AMERICA

YEAR OF BIRTH: 1941
ALTER EGO: Steve Rogers
OCCUPATION: Crime-fighter (formerly freelance artist)
FIRST APPEARANCE IN A COMIC BOOK: *Captain America Comics #1*
  (March 1941)
SUPERPOWERS: Enhanced strength, speed, and agility; a unique shield used
  both as protection and as a weapon
ORIGIN OF SUPERPOWER: Taking of a superserum
ARCHENEMY: Red Skull
BASE OF OPERATIONS: New York City
MEMBERSHIP: The Avengers (formerly the Invaders)
CREATED BY: Jack Kirby and Joe Simon
FIRST DRAWN BY: Jack Kirby

JEWISH CONNECTION:

In *Captain America #245* (May 1980), Captain America tries to save Nazi war
criminal Doctor Klaus Mendelhaus from death at the hands of Nazi hunters
Aaron and Marie Heller and his own Jewish neighbor, Anna Kapplebaum.

THE TROUBLE WITH SUPER HEROES IS WHAT TO DO BETWEEN PHONE BOOTHS.

—Ken Kesey, author, *One Flew Over the Cuckoo's Nest*

On December 7, 1941, in a sneak attack, the Japanese bombed the American naval fleet stationed at Pearl Harbor, Hawaii, destroying five out of eight battleships and killing over 2,400 servicemen. That blistering attack united the nation. Before that infamous day, most Americans had been isolationists reluctant to participate in foreign entanglements like the war in Europe. Now the debate was over—it was time for America to face the Axis head on.

One colorful hero had already joined the battle. In March 1941, more than six months before Pearl Harbor, *Captain America Comics* had been unveiled. The front cover showed its titular hero punching Hitler straight in the face, sending the ridiculous-looking Fuhrer tumbling. With that single, unforgettable image, the Nazi ideal of the Aryan *ubermensch* was subverted. Captain America was the first comic book character to enlist in World War II, and he became an instant phenomenon.

Like his predecessors Superman and Batman, Captain America was also created by two young, second-generation Jewish artists, writer Joe Simon and writer-illustrator Jack Kirby. And they, too, infused their work with their Jewish heritage. However, Captain America was born not on make-believe planet Krypton or in fictional Gotham City but on Manhattan's Lower East Side, the very real center of American Jewish immigration and regeneration—and Kirby and Simon's home turf.

Comic book adventures offered a fantastic alternative to ghetto life on the overcrowded Lower East Side, where rundown tenement buildings faced noisy streets teeming with people, animals, and garbage. Brawling was commonplace. Kirby recalled, "Captain America was me, and I was Captain America. I saw him as part of me, and he always will be. In the fight scenes, when Cap used to take on seven men at once, and five bodies would fly around the room while he punched two in the jaw—that's how I remember the street fights from my childhood."[1]

Growing up in poverty, Kirby (born Jacob Kurtzberg) dreamed of being an artist but was forced to drop out of Brooklyn's Pratt Institute after only one day because of financial hardship. Instead, Kirby worked on newspaper comic strips under gentile-sounding pseudonyms such as Jack Curtis, Curt Davis, and Lance Kirby until he finally settled on the name Jack Kirby.

Kirby met his partner, Joe Simon, at Martin Goodman's Timely Comics, where the mostly Jewish staff openly despised Hitler. When Goodman saw the preliminary sketches for *Captain America*, he immediately gave Kirby and Simon their own comic book. The character was an instant hit, selling almost one million copies an issue. "The U.S. hadn't yet entered the war when Jack and I did *Captain America*, so maybe he was our way at lashing out against the Nazi menace. Evidently, Captain America symbolized the American people's sentiments. When we were producing *Captain America*, we were outselling *Batman, Superman,* and all the others,"[2] Simon later commented.

Captain America #1 (1941) introduces the superhero's alter ego, Steve Rogers. A sickly Depression-era child, Rogers loses his parents at a young age, then tries to enlist in the military. Too feeble to join the regular forces, Rogers volunteers for a top-secret military medical experiment known as Operation: Rebirth headed by Dr. Reinstein (a very Jewish name that sounds suspiciously like "Albert Einstein," an already wildly popular, if little understood, cultural icon in the real world). The doctor injects Rogers with Secret-Soldier Serum.

Unfortunately, a Nazi spy infiltrates the experiment and kills Dr. Reinstein, leaving Rogers as the serum's sole beneficiary. Hailed by the U.S. military as a superhuman savior, Rogers dons a patriotic costume of red, white, and blue with a star on the chest and stripes at the waist. As Captain America, Rogers's most important early assignment is to destroy his evil counterpart, a Nazi agent called the Red Skull.

In the original comic, the Red Skull was a traitorous aviation magnate; however, in the 1960s, Kirby and Jewish writer Stan Lee created a background story for the villain. In this revisionist tale, the Red Skull begins life as orphan Johann Schmidt, who is adopted by a kindly old Jewish shopkeeper and his daughter. In an unprovoked act, Schmidt murders the young woman, then blames his adoptive family for his failings. After Hitler takes him under his wing, Schmidt is transformed into the Red Skull, the comic book personification of Nazi atrocities.

Captain America is no solitary superhero. He was soon partnered with the young Bucky Barnes. This partnership is certainly in the Judaic tradition of fruitful, dynamic partnerships. However, it is more likely that the introduction of Bucky was actually an attempt to duplicate the success of two other Jewish artists, Bill Finger and Bob Kane, who had recently written the popular Robin character into *Batman* for National Periodical Publications (later known as Detective Comics).

Nevertheless, the impact of Simon and Kirby's Jewish identity on their creation is obvious in other ways. In 1941, Jews throughout the Third Reich were forced to wear a yellow Star of David. That same year, the first gassing experiments were conducted at Auschwitz and 33,771 Jews were killed by Germans and Ukrainians at Babi Yar outside Kiev.

At the beginning of the war, the U.S. media rarely reported or even knew about these horrific events, but word of Jewish suffering at the hands of the Nazis trickled down to Kirby, Simon, and other Diaspora Jews in the form of wrenching letters from relatives trapped in the old country. Simon and Kirby used Captain America to strike back and boost American morale while proudly alluding to their religious faith. In a later issue, Steve Rogers watches newsreels depicting Nazi atrocities—newsreels Kirby and Simon surely must have watched as well.

Captain America's weapon of choice was a strange one—not a machine gun, but a shield. The shield is a famous Jewish symbol, the Magen David, which means the "Shield of David." (It's also known as the "Star of David" because the Magen David is a hexagram.) The term "shield" in Jewish prayer denotes the closeness and protection of God. In a sad twist of fate, Captain America's costume featured a star at the same time that Simon and Kirby's European brethren were being forced to wear a star of a very different kind.

Of course, a more literal reading of the costume is that it is the American flag brought to life. Captain America's star is, after all, five-pointed, not six-pointed like the Star of David. The flag-as-costume notion reinforces the ideal of assimilation. By literally cloaking their character in patriotism, Kirby and Simon became true Americans.

Despite its patriotic appearance, Captain America's costume also denotes deeply rooted mystical traditions. Along with other Jewish-penned superheroes, Captain America was in part an allusion to the Golem, the legendary creature said to have been constructed by the sixteenth-century mystic Rabbi Judah Loew to defend the Jews of medieval Prague. "The Golem was very much the precursor of the Superhero in that in every society there's a need for mythological characters, wish fulfillment. And the wish fulfillment in the Jewish case of the hero would be someone who could protect us. This kind of storytelling seems to dominate in Jewish culture,"[3] commented Will Eisner.

According to tradition, a golem is sustained by inscribing the Hebrew word *emet* (truth) upon its forehead. When the first letter is removed, leaving the word *met* (death), the golem will be destroyed. *Emet* is spelled with the letters *aleph*, *mem*, and *tav*. The first letter, *aleph*, is also the first letter of the Hebrew alphabet, the equivalent of the letter *A*. Captain America wears a mask with a white *A* on his forehead—the very letter needed to empower the golem.

Mask-wearing has long been associated with many classic (and not so classic) superheroes. Perhaps the mask symbolizes the desire of comic book creators who came from unassimilated Yiddish-speaking homes to explore dual identities. The notion of superheroes with dual identities undoubtedly mirrors their creators' own experiences as ethnic minority members with American alter egos. "Having a dual identity, changing your name and wearing a mask, of assimilating and reinventing yourself—it's impossible not to see these things as allegorical of the immigrant experience,"[4] commented novelist and comic book historian Michael Chabon.

The Bible is filled with stories of double identities and deceit. As Isaac lies blind on his deathbed, he is tricked by his son Jacob. Rebecca, Jacob's mother, uses goat skins to cover Jacob's smooth skin and to disguise him as his older brother, the hairy Esau. Later, Jacob himself is duped by his father-in-law when Jacob ends up married to the veiled (that is, masked) Leah and not his beloved Rachel.

Another biblical precursor of Kirby and Simon's creation is the young Hebrew shepherd David, who defeated the Philistine giant Goliath while armed with only his staff, his sling, and a few stones. Likewise, Kirby and Simon, armed with only a pencil and ink, were taking on the Nazis, a mighty Goliath of their time. Will Eisner confirmed this notion, commenting, "All of Jewish cultural history has been based around Jewish cultural fighters, like Samson and David. Now, in the 40s, we were facing the Nazis, an apparently unstoppable force. And what better way to deal with a supervillain like Hitler than with a superhero?"[5]

Captain America #6 (1941) echoes the David and Goliath story. In this issue, set in the Lower East Side, the Captain teams up with Bucky Barnes's classmates, the self-proclaimed Sentinels of Liberty. Captain

America discovers that the boys' teacher, Professor Hall, is really the sinister Camera Fiend and the school janitors are his henchmen. The Sentinels leap into action to save Captain America after he is knocked to the ground. When Barnes blows a whistle, the boys shout, "Bucky's battle whistle! Come on boys, the fight's on!"[6] Armed with rulers, blackboard erasers, and their fists, the boys beat the evildoers within an inch of their lives. The fight is vivid and violent, evoking the brawls Kirby experienced as a child in New York. The story's message is clear: the Jewish boys from the Lower East Side are ready to defend America.

Captain America #8 (1941) harkens back to Jewish slavery in ancient Egypt. A magical gem known as the Ruby of the Nile brings the mummified Pharaoh back to life, and like a modern-day Moses, Captain America is dispatched to destroy him. The Exodus was a favorite theme of Kirby's, one he returned to again and again in his work. In his personal life, Kirby enjoyed inviting guests to his home for a Passover Seder, the Jewish service that commemorates the Israelites' Exodus from Egypt. During the Seder, Jews read from a small book known as the Haggadah. (Interestingly, the Haggadahs used in Kirby's youth were cheaply mass produced and well illustrated, much like comic books!)

The intriguing story is told that as a boy, Kirby lay dying of pneumonia. Because the medicines of the day were scarce and expensive (not to mention barely effective), rabbis were called in to chant a kabbalistic exorcism in an effort to save him. As Kirby grew older, the impact of this dramatic event became apparent, and he acknowledged the biblical subtexts in his work. Kirby's nephew Robert Katz commented, "He did a whole Biblical sequence in pencil, Joshua at the battle of Jericho."[7] A drawing of Kirby's later creation, the Hulk, sporting a *tallit* (a prayer shawl), and yarmulke (the traditional Jewish male's head covering), hangs in the room of Katz's son.

"He was a very proud Jew," recalled Shimon Paskow, rabbi emeritus of California's Thousand Oaks Synagogue, where Kirby's name is on the wall. "I used to have members read the Torah portion. He always showed up. He took it very seriously." Paskow presided over "Kirby's colorful funeral, attended by an eclectic assortment of cartoonists, bikers and bohemians."[8]

But Kirby and Simon's creation, *Captain America*'s Steve Rogers, looked so Aryan with his blue eyes and blond hair. Why?

By projecting their own desires for assimilation onto their creations, young artists such as Kirby and Simon created an American ideal they saw as authentic. Cartoonist R. C. Harvey commented on a similar situation within the Hollywood studio establishment of the time, which consisted almost entirely of Jewish businessmen: "The America they portrayed in their films was the America they dreamed of belonging to. But it was not the actual America. It was however, so compelling a portrait, so vivid an impersonation, that all moviegoers, all Americans bought into it."[9] Jewish movie moguls Sam Goldwyn and Louis B. Mayer bankrolled patriotic fare like *Yankee Doodle Dandy*, changed the names of Jewish actors (Edward G. Robinson was born Emanuel Goldenberg, for instance), and made Danny Kaye bleach his hair. In the same way, meanwhile, Warner Brothers somehow managed to film *The Life of Emile Zola* without ever mentioning that Colonel Dreyfus was a Jew! Ironically, decades later, middle America eagerly embraced the idiosyncratic Jewish New Yorker, turning Woody Allen, Neil Simon, Mel Brooks, and Jerry Seinfeld into superstars.

Simon and Kirby's *Captain America* brought hope and inspiration to GIs on the front lines, who often spent their rare spare time reading comic books. An incredible one in four magazines shipped to troops abroad was a comic. Kirby explained, "I found a way to help the war effort by portraying the times in the form of comic characters. I was saying what was on my mind and I felt extremely patriotic."[10] This is all the more impressive because in the first few years of the war, it actually looked as if the Nazis would win. Images of Superman punching out a U-boat or Captain America tying a knot in a tank were welcome expressions of wish fulfillment.

Like that of Superman's Siegel and Shuster, Simon and Kirby's frontal assault on Hitler did not go unnoticed by the Nazis. In his biography of Kirby, Ronin Ro recounts a remarkable story of Nazi retribution against Simon and Kirby on American soil. The German-American Bund, a New York–based group that supported (and even dressed like) Hitler, objected to the pair's depiction of Nazis as murderous villains.

The Bund bombarded Timely Comics with hate mail and death threats. Seeing strange men loitering outside their building on Forty-Second Street, Timely employees contacted the police. Suddenly, Joe Simon was summoned to the telephone, and Mayor Fiorello LaGuardia himself assured Simon, "You boys over there are doing a good job. The City of New York will see that no harm comes to you."[11]

On June 7, 1943, Kirby received a telegram ordering him to report for active duty. Now he would follow his famous alter ego's example and take on the Nazis for real, coming face to face with his own victimized people, whose pain and suffering was worse than anything the imagination of a comic illustrator could conjure up.

Kirby's skills as an artist proved extremely helpful to the Allies. Biographer Ro recounts the story of the lieutenant who approached the new recruit and asked,

"Are you Jack Kirby the artist?"

"Yes, Sir, I drew *Captain America*."

"Good . . . I am making you a scout. You can go into these towns that we don't have and see if there is anybody there, draw maps and pictures of what you see, and come back and tell us if you find anything."[12]

Kirby also saw action in the Normandy invasion. "In later life, Kirby was sometimes reticent in talking about his war years," writes Jeet Heer, "but the big booming machines that would loom so large in Kirby's postwar art were created by someone who had seen mechanized warfare at close hand."[13]

On the home front, Simon also used his artistic skills to help the war effort. Instead of being sent overseas, he was summoned to Washington, D.C., to illustrate recruiting guides for the Coast Guard Academy. Other Jewish artists who traded in their pencils for weapons included Irwin Hasen (the Green Lantern), Will Eisner (the Spirit), Dave Berg (Uncle Sam), Mort Weisinger (editor, DC Comics), and Stan Lee (editor, Timely Comics).

After the war, Simon and Kirby returned to their professions but discovered that superheroes were somewhat superfluous in peacetime. Captain America hung up his shield in 1949.

When the character was revived decades later by new artists, Jewish themes again came up. In *Captain America* #237 (1979), Steve Rogers meets a Holocaust survivor who recalls being rescued from the Diebenwald concentration camp by Captain America. The 1980s saw the debut of Steve's Jewish girlfriend, Bernie Rosenthal, who was once married to an activist in the Jewish Protection Agency (an allusion to the Jewish Defense League). In *Captain America* #275 (1982), Steve (as Captain America) is forced to intervene when a confrontation between the JPA and a neo-Nazi group turns violent.

Thus, the themes embodied by Superman, Batman, and Captain America—justice, vigilantism, and patriotism—continued to emerge, again and again, as a new generation of superheroes donned their masks and set about repairing the world.

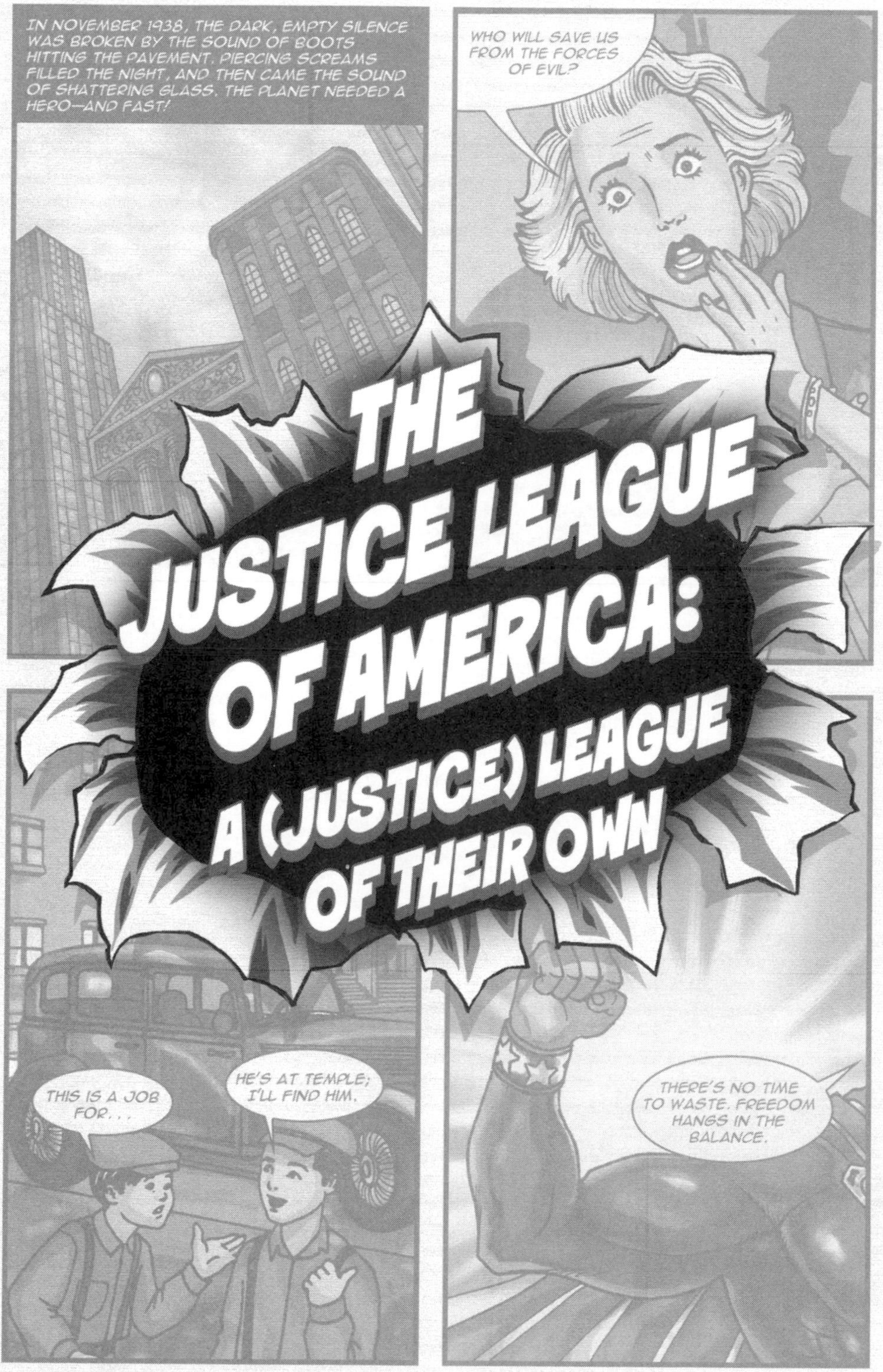
IN NOVEMBER 1938, THE DARK, EMPTY SILENCE WAS BROKEN BY THE SOUND OF BOOTS HITTING THE PAVEMENT. PIERCING SCREAMS FILLED THE NIGHT, AND THEN CAME THE SOUND OF SHATTERING GLASS. THE PLANET NEEDED A HERO—AND FAST!
WHO WILL SAVE US FROM THE FORCES OF EVIL?
THE JUSTICE LEAGUE OF AMERICA: A (JUSTICE) LEAGUE OF THEIR OWN
THIS IS A JOB FOR. . .
HE'S AT TEMPLE; I'LL FIND HIM.
THERE'S NO TIME TO WASTE. FREEDOM HANGS IN THE BALANCE.

SUPERHEROES

ATOM

YEAR OF BIRTH: 1961

ALTER EGO: Ray Palmer

OCCUPATION: Physicist

FIRST APPEARANCE IN A COMIC BOOK: *Showcase* #34 (October 1961)

SUPERPOWERS: A white-dwarf-star-powered device that alters height and weight

ORIGIN OF SUPERPOWER: Special lens that focuses ultraviolet light, along with an "x-factor" or "meta-gene" that prevents his atoms from becoming unstable when he changes height and weight

ARCHENEMY: Chronos

BASE OF OPERATIONS: Ivy Town, Connecticut

MEMBERSHIP: Teen Titans (formerly Suicide Squad and Justice League of America)

CREATED BY: Gardner Fox

FIRST DRAWN BY: Gil Kane

JEWISH CONNECTION:

In a special issue of *Justice League of America* (2004), a tribute to editor Julius Schwartz, Schwartz calls the brought-to-life superheroes "an octet of Gentiles," complaining that they're trying to guilt-whip a Jew. Without skipping a beat, Atom replies, "My mother was Jewish."

IF I WERE ASKED TO EXPRESS IN A SINGLE SENTENCE WHAT HAS HAPPENED TO MANY AMERICAN CHILDREN, I WOULD SAY THAT THEY WERE CONQUERED BY SUPERMAN.

—Dr. Fredric Wertham, author,
Seduction of the Innocent

In the early 1950s, superheroes faced their most deadly villain of all time. Dr. Fredric Wertham, a diminutive Freudian psychiatrist from Harlem, didn't look very menacing. But beneath that harmless exterior lurked a fanatical crusader. In his 1954 book, *Seduction of the Innocent*, Wertham claimed he'd discovered "a frightening correlation between comic book reading and juvenile delinquency." The dust jacket blared: "90,000,000 comic books are read each month. You think they are mostly about floppy-eared bunnies, attractive little mice and chipmunks? Go take a look."[1]

Among other claims, Wertham asserted that Superman was a fascist and that Batman and Robin's relationship was, well, less than kosher. In the book's introduction, Wertham asked,

Why does our civilization give to the child not its best but its worst, in paper, in language, in art, in ideas? What is the social meaning of these supermen, superwomen, super-lovers, super-boys, supergirls, super-ducks, super-mice, super-magicians, super-safecrackers?

How did Nietzsche get into the nursery?[2]

The blockbuster book was excerpted in *Reader's Digest* and *Ladies' Home Journal*, influencing millions of panic-stricken Americans. In some states, comic books were publicly burned. Wertham's crusade against the comic book industry eventually rocketed all the way to the U.S. Senate.

Under incredible pressure from the Senate and the general public to tone down their publications, comic book publishers brought in the voluntary Comics Code to censor themselves before they were forced out of business entirely. Horror and crime comics vanished from newsstands, and other genres toned down the violence and gore. EC Comics, one of Wertham's favorite targets, stopped publishing entirely—except for a little humor comic published by a Jewish father and son team. It was called *MAD* and is famous to this day for its sly, Yiddish-tinged humor—and unrestrained contempt for know-it-all authorities.

Ironically, Wertham had some things in common with his superhero nemeses and their creators. The Jewish doctor had changed his name from Friedrich Wertheimer when he immigrated to America from Germany in the early 1920s. However, unlike the artists he opposed, he came from a wealthy family and was highly educated.

Wertham's crusade was not the only challenge that superheroes faced. Dozens of characters had debuted in the 1940s, but by the early 1950s, many had become extinct. After all, the world had become a safer place after World War II, and their powers were no longer needed. Readers embraced other comic book genres, including those derided by Wertham: horror, science fiction, crime, romance, westerns, and funny animal stories.

The dirty business of saving the world was left to old stalwarts such as Superman, Batman, and Wonder Woman, who remained the only functioning superheroes in the DC Comics line. In the crazy climate of the times, DC publisher Jack Liebowitz was too nervous to release new titles, so editorial director Irwin Donenfeld came up with a fiscally responsible compromise: *Showcase*, a vehicle to test new characters before giving them their own titles.

The first three issues of *Showcase* met with mediocre success. Then issue #4, which reintroduced the 1940s character the Flash, was a smash hit. Superheroes could be popular in peacetime after all.

The man behind the new Flash was editor Julius Schwartz. Comic book historians agree that Schwartz's success with the Flash rejuvenated the entire industry and ushered in the Silver Age of comics. (The Golden Age of comics, which began in 1938, marked the birth of the genre. The Silver Age—from the mid-1950s until the early 1970s—saw superheroes become more human and multidimensional, as a character's particular mythos and personality became just as important as plot and action, if not more so.)

In his autobiography, *Man of Two Worlds*, Schwartz jokingly noted, "My parents, Joseph and Bertha were of Jewish descent, and emigrated from a small town outside Bucharest in Romania to come to the land of milk and honey—which other people have chosen to call the Bronx."[3] The Schwartzes, like millions of other Jews, saw America as a Golden *medina* (Yiddish for "golden land") and embraced American culture. As a child, Schwartz had two great passions: he was "the world's biggest baseball fan" (legend has it he teethed on a Yankees pennant) and "the world's biggest science fiction fan."[4]

Had he done nothing else, Schwartz would be fondly remembered today in the world of comics and fandom as the cofounder of the world's first science fiction fanzine in 1932. He produced the *Time Traveler* with fellow Jewish boys Allen Glasser, Forrest J. Ackerman, and Mortimer Weisinger. In those days, it was a small world for those with big imaginations: Schwartz later noted that "among the *Time Traveler*'s first subscribers was a fellow named Jerome Siegel from Cleveland."[5]

Along with Weisinger, Schwartz also cofounded the first science fiction literary agency, Solar Sales Service. Among their first clients was a youngster named Ray Bradbury. Schwartz also worked with Jewish science fiction writer extraordinaire Isaac Asimov.

Ironically, Schwartz, who is regarded by many as the greatest editor in the business, came into comics by default. Schwartz had absolutely no interest in comics but was astute enough to realize there was money to be made. Amazingly, he only bought his first comic book on the way to his job interview with DC Comics' Sheldon Mayer: "On my way to the subway I went to the newsstand and picked up three *All American Comics.* They cost a dime a piece back then . . . it turned out to be the best investment in my life."[6]

Hiring Schwartz turned out to be a great investment for DC, too. Schwartz's lifelong passion for science fiction sent the Flash in an exciting new direction that readers loved. The Flash is the alter ego of Barry Allen, a police scientist doused in a dangerous electrified concoction after lightning strikes a rack of chemicals. The accident gives Allen the ability to run at superspeed, a gift he uses to aid the police in fighting crime.

Believe it or not, the notion of superspeed is rooted in biblical lore. God has granted a few righteous people the power to travel, quite literally, faster than a speeding bullet. The Talmud highlights the stories of individuals who possessed the supernatural power known as *kefitzat ha-Derekh* (meaning "the jumping of the road").

The Bible recounts the story of Abraham, who sent his servant Eliezer to Canaan to find a wife for his son Isaac. Eliezer made the journey, which normally took about a week by camel, in only a few hours. The famous tenth-century Bible commentator Rabbi Solomon ben Isaac, known as Rashi, notes that Eliezer experienced *kefitzat ha-Derekh*, which enabled him to travel from Charan to Canaan in a single day.

When Eliezer recounts that day's events, he omits the supernatural aspect of his journey. Eliezer deemed his superpowers unimportant and

The ultimate superhero fantasy? Simon and Kirby never got close enough to Hitler to sock him in the jaw, but they drew their hero doing just that. Amazingly, this issue appeared months before America went to war with Germany!

Captain America Comics #1 (March 1941) ©2006 Marvel Characters, Inc. Used with permission. Art by Jack Kirby.

Good thing he's already circumcised! The Thing's Jewish roots are revealed for the first time in this memorable issue.

"Remembrance of Things Past," *Fantastic Four* (3rd series) #56 (August 2002), ©2006 Marvel Characters, Inc. Used with permission.
Art by Stuart Immonen.

"Remembrance of Things Past," *Fantastic Four* (3rd series) #56 (August 2002), ©2006 Marvel Characters, Inc. Used with permission.
Art by Stuart Immonen.

"Remembrance of Things Past," *Fantastic Four* (3rd series) #56 (August 2002), ©2006 Marvel Characters, Inc. Used with permission.
Art by Stuart Immonen.

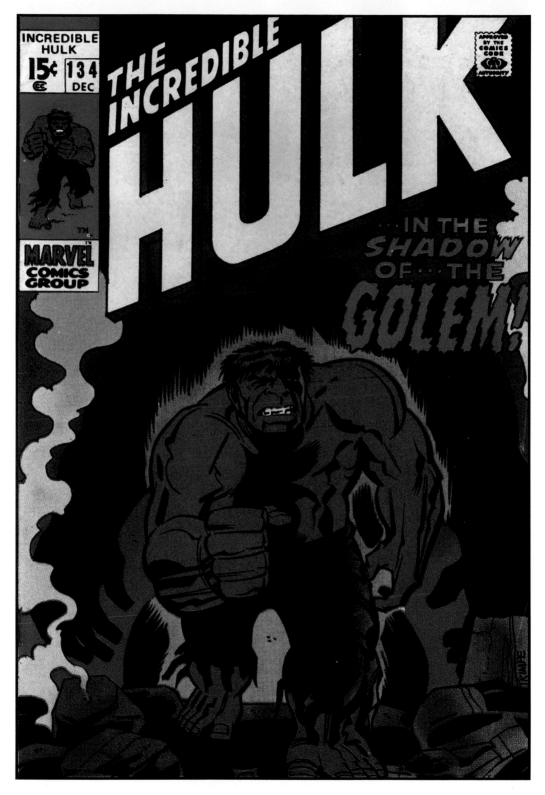

No golem actually appears in this issue, but the similarities between the Hulk and the legendary golem are quite clear.

Bruce Banner (the Hulk's alter ego) befriends an Arab boy who is later killed by a terrorist bomb. Israeli superheroine Sabra mistakenly believes the Hulk is to blame, and a battle ensues.

"Power in the Promised Land," *The Incredible Hulk* #256 (February 1981), ©2006 Marvel Characters, Inc. Used with permission.
Art by Sal Buscema.

The Hulk gets a close-up view of the Western Wall while Sabra pummels him with both powerful punches and vicious metaphors.

The Incredible Hulk #387 (November 1991) ©2006 Marvel Characters. Used with permission.
Written by Peter David, illustrated by Dale Keown and Josef Rubinstein.

As if Spider-Man doesn't have enough angst already—now an old Jewish tailor is kvetching about his costume.

"You Want Pants with That?" *Amazing Spider-Man* #502 (February 2004), ©2006 Marvel Characters, Inc. Used with permission.
Art by John Romita, Jr.

"You Want Pants with That?" *Amazing Spider-Man* #502 (February 2004), ©2006 Marvel Characters, Inc.
Used with permission.
Art by John Romita, Jr.

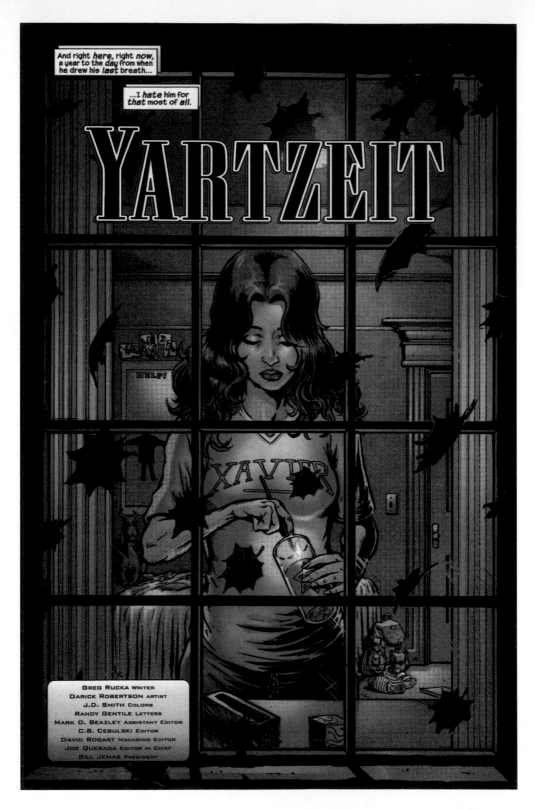

After the death of her boyfriend, Colossus, a grieving Kitty Pryde lights the traditional Yartzeit candle, the Jewish memorial candle that burns for twenty-four hours.

"Yartzeit" *X-Men Unlimited* #38 (November 2002), ©2006 Marvel Characters, Inc. Used with permission. Art by Darick Robertson.

"Yartzeit" *X-Men Unlimited* #38 (November 2002), ©2006 Marvel Characters, Inc. Used with permission. Art by Darick Robertson.

In this issue of the *X-Men*, Jewish characters Kitty Pryde (Shadowcat) and Magneto attend a gathering of Holocaust survivors at the National Holocaust Memorial in Washington, D.C.

"The Spiral Path," *The Uncanny X-Men* #199 (November 1985), ©2006 Marvel Characters, Inc. Used with permission.
Art by John Romita, Jr., and Dan Green.

chose to act in secret. The Flash also conceals his true power through a disguise and lives a clandestine existence.

◆ ● ◆

After the Flash, the next in line for a postwar makeover was the Green Lantern, originally coscripted by Bill Finger. When it came time to draw the Green Lantern's Guardians of the Universe (a tribe of identical short, blue aliens), artist Gil Kane (born Eli Katz) modeled them after Israeli prime minister David Ben-Gurion. Schwartz noted, "We decided that all of the Guardians should look alike because basically in all comics *all* aliens look alike. Gil Kane then based their general appearance on the Prime Minister of Israel at the time."[7]

Schwartz was quietly proud of his Jewish roots. In "Remembering Julius Schwartz," comic book writer Elliot S. Maggin recounted his "favorite moment with Julie":

> I invited him over to my parents' house for their Passover Seder, the annual ritual dinner where you tell long stories about freedom and adventuring before you eat . . . Apparently Julie had not been to a Seder in a number of years . . . There's a crucial point at the beginning of the Seder ceremony when the youngest person at the table reads a short but rather difficult paragraph in Hebrew called the Four Questions . . . It fell to my youngest sister Robin to read the questions, and she never particularly enjoyed the role . . .
>
> "I haven't been to Hebrew school since 1928," Julie barked. "And watch this." He read the Four Questions in perfect Hebrew, beginning to end, without tripping over a syllable. So it was that the oldest person at the table asked the Four Questions this time. My father was thrilled—it brought us an entire whining-session closer to the food.
>
> A few days later, back at work, he showed me a gold watch he'd gotten for being the smartest kid in the Hebrew school he attended. It had Hebrew

letters for the numbers, and I suggested it ought to run counter-clockwise [the Hebrew alphabet runs right to left] but it didn't.[8]

After the success of the Flash and the Green Lantern, Schwartz began his most ambitious project yet: the Justice League of America. A revamped version of the old Justice Society of America, the Justice League was the world's first superhero group and included the biggest *machers* (leaders) of its day (that is, those contracted to DC Comics). This superhero team demonstrated that while they were super on their own, together these heroes were even more super.

Schwartz felt that "society" was "a quiet word," pointing out that readers were more familiar with the word "league" thanks to baseball's National and American Leagues (not to mention the Jewish Defense League). And so the revamped Justice League debuted in *The Brave and the Bold* #28 (1960). The original lineup consisted of Aquaman, Wonder Woman, Superman, the Green Lantern, Batman, the Flash, and J'onn J'onzz. That first issue included the Justice League of America's mission statement: "Foes of evil! Enemies of injustice! To the mighty heroes of the Justice League of America all wrong-doing is a menace to be stamped out—whether it comes from outer space— from the watery depths of the seven seas—or springs full-blown from the minds of men!"[9]

The Bible also emphasizes the virtue of justice, commenting, "Justice, justice shall you pursue."[10] The word "justice" (*tzedek* in Hebrew) is famously repeated. Why? One reason is to magnify the special emphasis placed upon evenhandedness.

The very notion of an entire league of heroes also fits well with biblical archetypes. While Judaism has its roots in the accomplishments of powerful patriarchs and matriarchs, a special emphasis is also placed upon the tribe: the synthesis of everyone's talents for the greater good.

The twelve tribes of Israel have their origins in Jacob's sons. Each son is entrusted with a particular power that will dictate his tribe's distinct role in the history of the Jewish people. The Hebrew word for tribes, *shevatim*, means a "branch," alluding to their separate yet united nature.

Two centuries later, before their entry into the Holy Land of Israel, the twelve tribes were blessed by Moses. Each tribe had retained its distinct identity, and the Jewish people remained a cohesive nation. Each tribe had its own leader, a designated location where it could camp around the Tabernacle, a color and flag, and a representative stone on the high priest's ceremonial breastplate. Similarly, the Justice League worked together, but members kept their own identity and wore their own costumes rather than a Justice League uniform.

The Justice League teaches that not even superheroes live in a vacuum. Sometimes they have to rely on their fellow supercolleagues to assist them when the going gets tough. In the same way, Moses enlists his own supersquad after he leads the Israelites out of bondage and they are attacked by Amalek. The Bible recounts:

> Amalek came and battled Israel at Rephidim. Moses said to Joshua, "Choose people for us and go do battle with Amalek. Tomorrow I will stand on top of the hill with the staff of God in my hand." Joshua did as Moses said to him, to do battle with Amalek; and Moses, Aaron, and Hur ascended to the top of the hill. It happened that when Moses raised his hand up, Israel prevailed, and when he let his hand down, Amalek prevailed. Moses' hands grew heavy. So they took a stone and put it under him, and he sat on it; and Aaron and Hur supported his hands, one on this side and one on that side, and he remained with his hands in faithful prayer until sunset. Joshua weakened Amalek and its people with the sword's blade.[11]

According to the sages, the Jews were actually attacked because they lacked unity. This is alluded to in the very name of the location where the battle occurred—Refidim—a name that is etymologically related to the Hebrew word *pirud*, meaning "disunity." Only through teamwork are battles won.

The first issue of the new *Justice League* comic sees our heroes seated in a semicircle around an oval table. The scene is reminiscent of the Sanhedrin, the ancient Jewish court system that consisted of seventy-one judges. The Sanhedrin also sat in a semicircle so all members could see each other and have an equal view of all witnesses. They were required to hear all testimony directly and understand every language spoken by Jews around the world. Every member of the Sanhedrin was also distinguished in Torah knowledge and secular disciplines.

In the 1970s, the Justice League welcomed its smallest member: the Atom. The Atom also happens to be the tiniest Jewish character in comics! In *Justice League of America* #188 (first series, 1981), the Atom spends Hanukkah with his superhero friends. The League's satellite is attacked and its life-support systems fail. Miraculously, the oxygen supply lasts long enough for repairs to be made. The Atom compares that miracle with the miracle of Hanukkah.

In the 1980s, the Atom's superhero godson joined the Justice League. Known as the Atom Smasher (or Nuklon), Albert Rothstein is a strapping seven foot six inches, a "nice Jewish boy" who celebrates Hanukkah with his widowed mother. In *Justice League of America* #95 (second series, 1995), Nuklon is forced to rebuff the advances of the beautiful Fire:

> *Nuklon:* "Fire . . . Bea . . . I'm really . . . really flattered. But I'm going to marry a Jewish girl."
> *Fire:* "Who is she?!"
> *Nuklon*: "I haven't met her yet!"
> *Fire:* "You—?! What is this, some kind of arranged marriage thing?"
> *Nuklon:* "No, no, no! I mean I don't know who I'll marry yet. I just know she'll have to be Jewish. You see, it isn't just my happiness that matters. I owe something to my family . . . to my heritage. I'm like a link in a chain. I can't be the one to break that chain. So . . . I'm sorry, Bea. Unless you want to convert?!"[12]

Another example of teamwork in action was in DC's *Legion of Super-Heroes*. The series is set in the thirtieth century and was conceived as a vehicle for Superboy. In the first issue, Lightning Boy, Saturn Girl, and Cosmic Boy travel back in time to recruit Superboy as a member of their crime-fighting Legion. Over the years, the number of Legionnaires increased. One character in particular stands out: Colossal Boy.

Colossal Boy's real name was Gim Allon. Gim had been vacationing on Mars when he was bathed in meteoric radiation, leaving him with the power to grow at will. Colossal Boy can grow to some twenty-five feet tall, with a corresponding increase in strength and mass. In *Christmas with the Super-Heroes #1* (1988), it is revealed that Gim was born in Israel and spent his summers in a kibbutz.

In the 1980s, DC Comics publisher and writer Paul Levitz began to ponder Colossal Boy's real name and was struck by its resemblance to that of former Israeli cabinet minister Yigal Allon, who had mapped the strategy for the Six-Day War.

Inspired, Levitz expanded Colossal Boy's backstory in *Legion of Super-Heroes #308* (1984). When Gim Allon introduces his beautiful (albeit orange) alien wife, Year, to his parents, Gim's mother asks his father, "Now, I wonder if I can find a way to convince them to bring their kids up Jewish?"[13]

It was a conversation that the Jewish founders of Golden and Silver Age comics would have found extraordinary, an indication of the growing confidence that latter-day Jewish comic creators had in openly celebrating their faith. Julius Schwartz's opinion about this new take on Colossal Boy has not been recorded, but it is easy to imagine the man with the Hebrew-school watch being pleased.

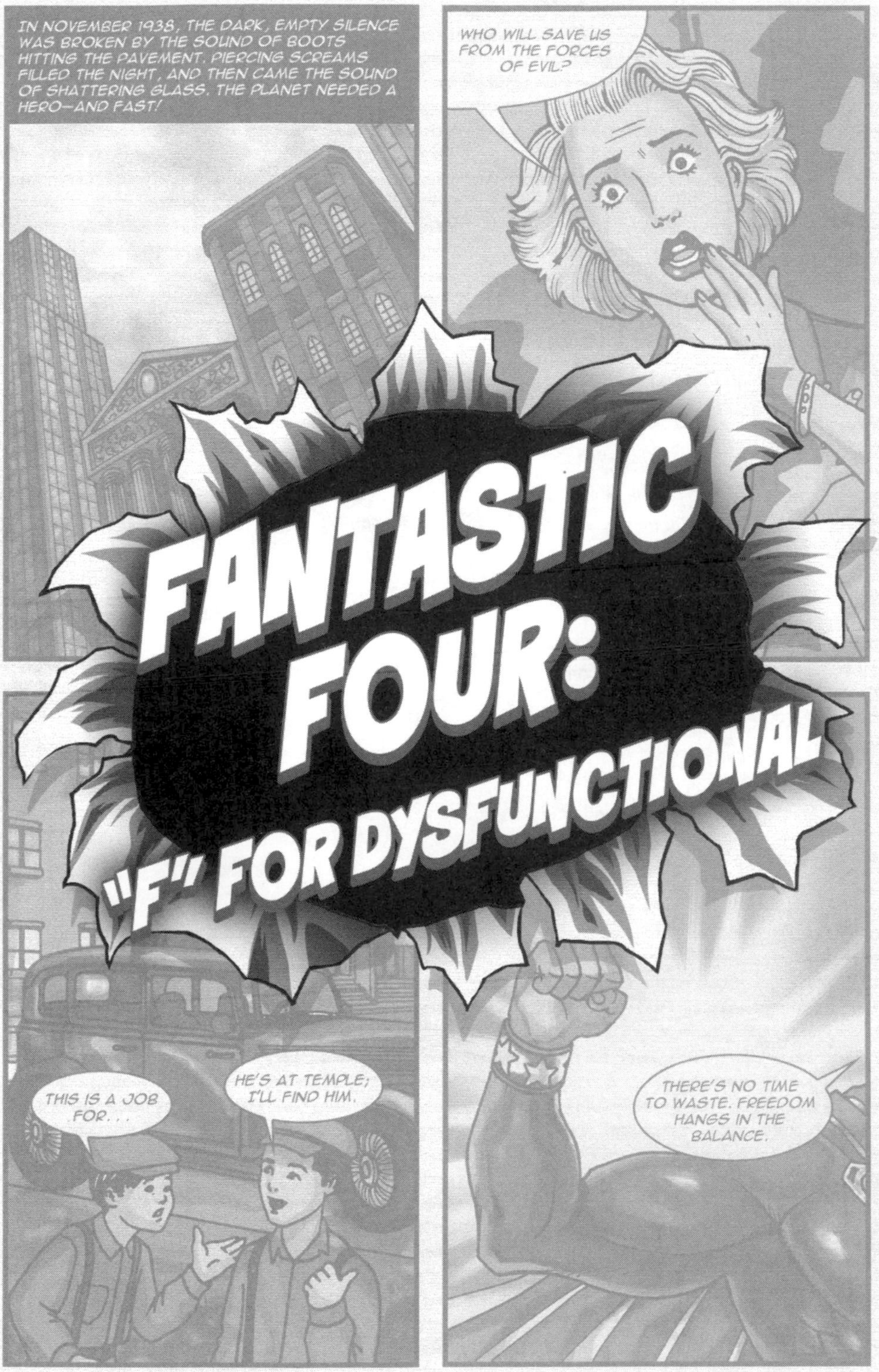
IN NOVEMBER 1938, THE DARK, EMPTY SILENCE WAS BROKEN BY THE SOUND OF BOOTS HITTING THE PAVEMENT. PIERCING SCREAMS FILLED THE NIGHT, AND THEN CAME THE SOUND OF SHATTERING GLASS. THE PLANET NEEDED A HERO—AND FAST!
WHO WILL SAVE US FROM THE FORCES OF EVIL?
FANTASTIC FOUR:
"F" FOR DYSFUNCTIONAL
THIS IS A JOB FOR. . .
HE'S AT TEMPLE; I'LL FIND HIM.
THERE'S NO TIME TO WASTE. FREEDOM HANGS IN THE BALANCE.

SUPERHEROES

THING

YEAR OF BIRTH: 1961

ALTER EGO: Benjamin Jacob Grimm

OCCUPATION: Superhero, professional adventurer (formerly wrestler and test pilot)

FIRST APPEARANCE IN A COMIC BOOK: *Fantastic Four #1* (November 1961)

SUPERPOWERS: Enhanced strength and invulnerability

ORIGIN OF SUPERPOWER: Exposure to cosmic rays

ARCHENEMY: Dr. Doom

BASE OF OPERATIONS: New York

MEMBERSHIP: Fantastic Four

CREATED BY: Stan Lee

FIRST DRAWN BY: Jack Kirby

JEWISH CONNECTION:

In the *Twisted Toyfare Theatre* story "Seder-Masochism," reprinted in *Twisted Toyfare Theatre* volume 1 (2003), the Thing becomes so bored during the telling of the Passover story that he decides to speed up events in the story. Ignoring *Star Trek's* "prime directive," he uses a time machine to go back in time and change history by freeing the slaves himself.

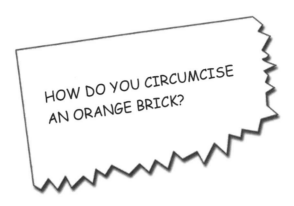

HOW DO YOU CIRCUMCISE AN ORANGE BRICK?

—Sign in the window of Cosmic Comics

Manhattan's Cosmic Comics posed the above strange question in its store window in the summer of 2002. At the same time, Internet fan sites were buzzing with other less-than-kosher questions about the Sabbath obligations of superheroes. The reason? A beloved comic book character had finally come out of the spiritual closet. The Thing, of all things, was Jewish.

The Thing is the pumpkin-colored cinderblock member of the Fantastic Four, the superhero team created by writer Stan Lee and artist Jack Kirby for Marvel Comics in 1961. In those days, the Thing's religion was the last thing on the creators' minds. They were just trying to outdo their comic book competition.

Rival publisher DC Comics was enjoying phenomenal success with its new *Justice League of America* series, which brought together DC's Golden Age favorites—Superman, Batman, Wonder Woman, the Flash, and the Green Lantern—into one exciting (and profitable) package.

Marvel Comics chief, Martin Goodman, charged Lee and Kirby with recreating DC's blockbuster brainstorm for Marvel.

There was a catch. DC was Marvel's only competitor, but it also owned National, Marvel's distributor. Any comic that copied DC products too closely would be instantly vetoed. Since DC superheroes were typically costumed and masked and had secret identities, Kirby and Lee were obliged to work outside these firmly established conventions and come up with something highly original yet enough like the Justice League to piggyback on its success.

The result? The Fantastic Four, a team of superheroes unlike any before. "I tried to make them like real people with their warts revealed. But beyond that, beneath all their bickering, I attempted to show that they genuinely cared for each other,"[1] said Lee. In other words, the Fantastic Four were a family.

Lee owed his very job to family: his cousin was Martin Goodman's wife. Lee's parents, Jack and Celia, had moved to Manhattan's Upper West Side from Romania in search of a better life, then suffered tremendously during the Depression. When the family's utilities were cut, Jack spent each day in a fruitless search for work. "I always felt sorry for my father . . . there were just no jobs to be had,"[2] Lee recalled. It was a feeling Lee's comic book contemporaries would have understood all too well, a sympathy for the underdog that manifested itself in their art.

Young Lee (then Lieber) immersed himself in books: first the escapist fiction of H. G. Wells, Arthur Conan Doyle, and Edgar Rice Burroughs, then everything from Shakespeare to the Bible. When he had no books, he read the labels on ketchup bottles.

The story of the Fantastic Four's origin is told in the very first issue. Pilot Ben Grimm, scientist Reed Richards, Reed's fiancée, Susan Storm, and her impetuous brother, Johnny, embark on a distinctly cold war, post-Sputnik adventure: to beat "the Commies" in the space race. On board a ship designed by Reed himself, the foursome are hit by powerful cosmic rays. Upon returning to Earth, the crew discovers that the rays have affected each of them differently. Reed, the leader of the group, becomes Mr. Fantastic, able to stretch his body; Susan (later Reed's wife) is now Invisible Girl (later Invisible Woman) and is placed second in command; Johnny sprouts flames and takes flight as a human fireball, becoming the Human Torch.

Ben Grimm is affected the most: his body turns into an orange, rocklike substance. Superstrong yet disfigured, he ruefully calls himself the Thing.

Unlike previous superheroes, the Fantastic Four did not rely on double identities and disguises. In their alternative world, they were high-profile celebrities headquartered in the Baxter Building on New York's Fifth Avenue. They got fan mail by the sackload and were mobbed at the airport (a little like the other "Fab Four," their real-life contemporaries, the Beatles).

Each member of the Fantastic Four reacts differently to his or her new powers. The youthful Human Torch at first uses his new abilities to show off. In *Fantastic Four* #16 (1963), he enlivens a high school gathering by writing the words "Go Glenville High" in fire across the sky. (This was perhaps a homage to the original flying superhero, Superman, whose creators, Siegel and Shuster, attended Glenville High and wrote for its paper, the *Glenville Torch*.)

In *Fantastic Four* #3 (1962), Susan becomes practical and maternal, designing costumes for the Four. "If we're in this business of crime fighting for real, if we're a team, we should look like a team!" she exclaims. The Thing lets out a kvetch: "Costumes . . . tights . . . that's kids' stuff! Who needs 'em???"[3]

The Thing had good reason to kvetch. As the only member who can't turn his powers on and off, the Thing will remain a physical freak for eternity, as well as a reluctant hero. In the very first issue, he declares: "You don't have to make a speech, big shot! We understand! We've gotta use that power to help mankind, right?"[4]

The Thing had questioned the safety of Reed's original mission all along, and these doubts led to an uncomfortable relationship between the two. Forever after, Reed harbored latent feelings of guilt, and Susan was often left to mediate.

The family dynamic was unmistakable from the start. Prior to the release of the *Fantastic Four*, the family unit had never been explored within the comic book genre. Superheroes tackled the dirty work of saving the world alone and worked together only out of necessity. The Fantastic Four were different. When Reed and Susan married, the team became, quite literally, a nuclear family in the nuclear age. Three of the four are directly related, with the Thing taking the role of crusty uncle, stubborn child, or bratty teen. The Justice League of America is a great superhero team, but the Fantastic Four are a great superhero family.

The family is the very heart of the Jewish community. It is the vessel through which moral values and spiritual practices have been handed down for thousands of years. Strong families build strong societies.

After the destruction of the holy Temple, the traditional Jewish home took on many of the Temple's functions. "Shalom Bayit" is the term given to the promotion of peace and harmony within the home. The Fantastic Four depict this ongoing struggle for peace within a family. While they are often, quite literally, at each other's throats, they're also willing to risk their lives for the safety of their "family."

Other Judaic themes are explored in the series, such as the biblical Exodus that so captivated Jack Kirby. In *Fantastic Four* #19 (1963), the foursome is enslaved by an evil Egyptian Pharaoh from the future—an atomic age twist on the stories in the Bible. The issue's front cover portrays the Fantastic Four enslaved by abusive taskmasters. Soon the Thing regains his power and tears down the pillars of the palace. The scene mirrors that of Samson or perhaps Superman or even Superman mirroring Samson.

Mythologically, the Fantastic Four parallel the four classical building blocks of matter: earth, water, air, and fire. The Thing clearly possesses the characteristics of earth. Like water, Mr. Fantastic can change his shape and bend like a liquid. Invisible Girl, like air, is hidden even when present.

The association of the Human Torch with fire is obvious. These elements also figure prominently in Jewish spiritual practices: lighting candles (fire), blowing the *shofar,* or ram's horn (air), immersing oneself in the ritual *mikvah* bath (water), and burying damaged sacred texts (earth).

Just as the Fantastic Four function as a family unit, which seems to denote completeness, so too the number four is symbolic of completion. A year has four seasons, a month has four weeks, a compass has four directions, and so on.

The number four is also a recurring symbol in Judaism. Examples include the story of the four sons, the four cups of wine, and the four questions, all from the Passover service (a Kirby favorite). Judaism has four matriarchs—Sarah, Rebecca, Rachael, and Leah—and the Kabbalah speaks of the four mystical worlds.

Over the years, Fantastic Four fans have felt particular affection for the misunderstood creature the Thing. The Thing has extreme strength, is impervious to bullets, and can endure intense physical pain. He is not immune to emotional pain, however. A skilled pilot and former college roommate of Reed's, the Thing blames his friend for his accursed condition, which has left him angry, vulnerable, and shy. Beneath his disfigurement, the Thing possesses a heart of gold (or maybe rock). Kirby admitted in interviews that the Thing was his alter ego, and Lee called the Thing "my favorite character of the Foursome."[5]

The Thing's real name is Benjamin Jacob Grimm. Born on the "earthy" Lower East Side of Manhattan, he belonged to the Yancy Street gang in his youth. Young Jack Kirby fought street gangs on the Lower East Side, too, where Delancey is the main street.

Ben's youth comes back to haunt him in the famous 2002 issue entitled "Remembrance of Things Past." In this issue, some forty years after the character's debut, the Thing's true Semitic identity is finally revealed.

That issue explored the experiences of both the Thing and American Jewry in considerable depth and sensitivity, even humor. In a flashback, Ben endures the death of his older brother, Danny. Police inform him that "God took him to a better place." Shortly after, Ben joins the Yancy Street gang. His initiation? Steal something from Mr. Sheckerberg's pawnshop. Ben returns with Mr. Sheckerberg's prized possession—his Star of David necklace.

The gang later rejects Ben when he leaves their neighborhood to become a pilot. In leaving the neighborhood, Ben leaves behind his Jewish identity. Historian Edward S. Shapiro has written that the success experienced by American Jews enabled them to move out of the tenements of their childhood: "The fervent desire of the first and second generations of East European Jews that their children not enter the sweat-shops or live in tenements has been fulfilled beyond their wildest expectations."[6] In search of the elusive American dream, Jews like Benjamin Grimm moved out of the ghettos and into the mainstream. Sadly, achieving this dream came at a price: the loss of much of their own Jewish heritage. Ben's theft of the Star of David represents the banishment of faith and symbolizes his willingness to betray his religion in exchange for a feeling of belonging, not to mention worldly success.

The story flashes forward to a modern-day Ben, now transformed into the Thing, as he passes by Sheckerberg's Pawnshop. Consumed with guilt, he enters the store, only to be set upon by a much older Mr. Sheckerberg, armed with a baseball bat. "Benjamin Jacob Grimm! You've only given me grief my whole life—why should now be any different?" asks Mr. Sheckerberg. Ben responds gruffly that "in case you ain't heard the news the last couple of years, I'm one of the good guys!"[7]

Ben vows to help Mr. Sheckerberg, who is being threatened by Ben's nemesis, the evil Powderkeg. Powderkeg and the Thing battle it out, and Mr. Sheckerberg is critically injured in the process. The Thing contemplates what can be done to save him. "Givin' him CPR could crush him." Then tapping into a place hidden deep within his consciousness, he remembers something. "There is one thing. Lessee, been a while . . . " Suddenly, the Pintele Yid is revealed as he declares, "*Sh'ma yisrael adonai eloheinu adonai echad . . .* uhm *. . . baruch shem k'vod malchuto l'olam va'ed.*"[8]

Translated as "Hear O Israel, the Lord our God, the Lord is One. Blessed is the Name of His glorious kingdom for all eternity," the Shema is the most famous of all Jewish prayers. This declaration of faith is said upon arising in the morning and retiring at night. It is the first prayer a Jewish child is taught and the last words a Jew recites before death. When the prayer is written inside a Torah scroll, the Hebrew letters *ayin* and *daled* of the first verse are enlarged—encoded to spell out the Hebrew word *aid*—"witness." Thus, by saying the Shema, the Thing is joining his Jewish brethren throughout the eons, testifying to the oneness of God.

Remarkably, Mr. Sheckerberg recovers. "It's good to see you haven't forgotten what you learned at Temple, Benjamin," the old man says. "All these years in the news, they never mention you're Jewish. I thought maybe you were ashamed of it a little?"[9]

Like the Thing, Jews have often turned to God in times of crisis. Like so many of his American tribesmen, the Thing hid his roots to avoid confrontation. "Figure there's enough trouble in this world without people thinkin' Jews are all monsters like me,"[10] he tells Mr. Sheckerberg poignantly.

The Thing proves the age-old Jewish adage that one can take the Jew out of Judaism but one cannot take Judaism out of the Jew. His confrontation with Powderkeg gives him his long-awaited chance to repent. Opening up his belt buckle, shaped like the number four, the Thing reveals the very Star of David necklace he'd stolen so many years ago. His true identity had been tucked away beneath his superhero costume all along.

Repentance (*teshuvah* in Hebrew) is a basic tenet of Judaism encouraging introspection and reconciliation with people we have hurt through our negative actions. *Teshuvah* is actually better translated as "return," not "repentance." Borscht belt jokes aside, guilt is not really a Jewish concept. Mistakes should be seen as opportunities for character and spiritual growth. Rabbi Moshe ben Maimon, an eleventh-century philosopher and physician known as Maimonides, stated, "*Teshuvah* brings near those who were distant. Yesterday was this man hateful before God—despicable, distant, and abominable. But today he is beloved and cherished, near and dear."[11] Yom Kippur, the day of atonement, is a day dedicated to *teshuvah*. Upon returning the stolen necklace, the Thing declares, "I thought maybe today was the day of atonement."

The issue ends as Mr. Sheckerberg harkens back to an ancient Jewish protector. "Remember the tale of the Golem, Benjamin? He was made of clay, but he wasn't a monster. He was a protector." The final panel depicts Powderkeg in police custody, shouting sarcastically to the Thing, "You don't look Jewish."[12]

This latter-day revelation of the Thing's ethnicity sparked passionate, thoughtful, and humorous debates among fans. Tom Brevoort, the non-Jewish editor who commissioned the script, did not realize the story would be a watershed moment in the medium, giving a long-overdue nod to all the Jews who'd helped create comics, beginning with Siegel and Shuster.

What made Brevoort see the Thing as Jewish, besides the name Benjamin Jacob Grimm and the character's Lower East Side origins? Brevoort admitted that an unpublished drawing of the Thing by Jack Kirby had confirmed his suspicions. "In [Jack Kirby's] home, over his hearth, he had done just for himself and his family a drawing of The Thing in a full rabbinical uniform with a yarmulke, and so forth."[13]

Brevoort continued: "His pre-Thing days that had been depicted had sort of the flavor of a typical Jewish immigrant family without ever actually coming out and saying so." Brevoort also saw the Thing as conforming to the Jewish archetype of the Golem made of clay.

Consider that Benjamin was the name of Kirby's father. Benjamin Kirby was a devout Jew who attended synagogue every single day and on weekends. Unlike his father, Jack Kirby attended only around the High Holidays, although he would say, "I love God, and I believe in God."[14]

The Thing's middle name is Jacob, Kirby's original name, changed later to Jack. Perhaps the name is also a reference to the biblical Jacob. Like the Thing, the Jewish patriarch Jacob was involved in brawling: he once spent an entire night wrestling with an angel.

Unfortunately, Kirby was no longer alive to comment in 2002, but Stan Lee, his partner, confessed that he personally never intended the Thing to be Jewish. He sounded flattered, if flustered, during a radio interview taped just after the release of "Remembrance": "You know, I didn't intend for him to be Jewish. No. I never thought for a minute what [the characters'] religions were."

The show's host pressed bravely on: "How much has Jewishness do you think informed the medium"?

Laughing, Lee replied: "You know, I have no idea. I never really thought of it . . . It is strange when you mention that the—perhaps best-known of all the characters—Spiderman, Superman and Batman were done by Jewish writers. I guess that is an odd thought." He added apologetically, "I hope I didn't ruin your whole show."[15]

Even at that late date, long after he'd changed his name from Lieber, Lee seemed compelled to play down his own Jewish background, let alone the Thing's. Like Bob Kane before him, Lee didn't directly address his Jewish heritage in his autobiography, *Excelsior* (except in an aside, where Lee calls his mother "a nice, rather old-fashioned Jewish lady"). In another interview, Lee had allowed that "Jewish culture is great, and I'm proud of it. Jewish people—and I include myself—I think we think a certain way, we feel a certain way, we react to things a certain way."[16]

The legacy of the Fantastic Four endures. The summer of 2005 saw the release of a *Fantastic Four* feature film. It was panned by critics but a smash hit with fans. The movie's producer and current Marvel chief, Avi Arad, hinted that the Thing's Jewish faith might be explored in sequels. (Arad himself is no stranger to superheroics. *Jerusalem Report* reporter Sheli Teitelbaum noted that Arad had "served as a lowly grunt during the Six-Day War, attached to an infantry unit tasked with holding down hard-won positions in Jerusalem."[17])

The success of the Thing proved that superheroes didn't have to follow the clean-cut, all-American model set down by Superman. The times were changing, and readers welcomed a reluctant hero like the Thing,

fantastic four

79

with his cynical wisecracks and deep emotional wounds. Stan Lee, Jack Kirby, and other comic book creators were happy to oblige. It was the 1960s. Assimilation was less of an issue now for these successful Jewish artists, and patriotism was increasingly viewed as a quaint, old-fashioned notion. Comic book heroes came to reflect those changes, perhaps none more than Stan Lee's next invention.

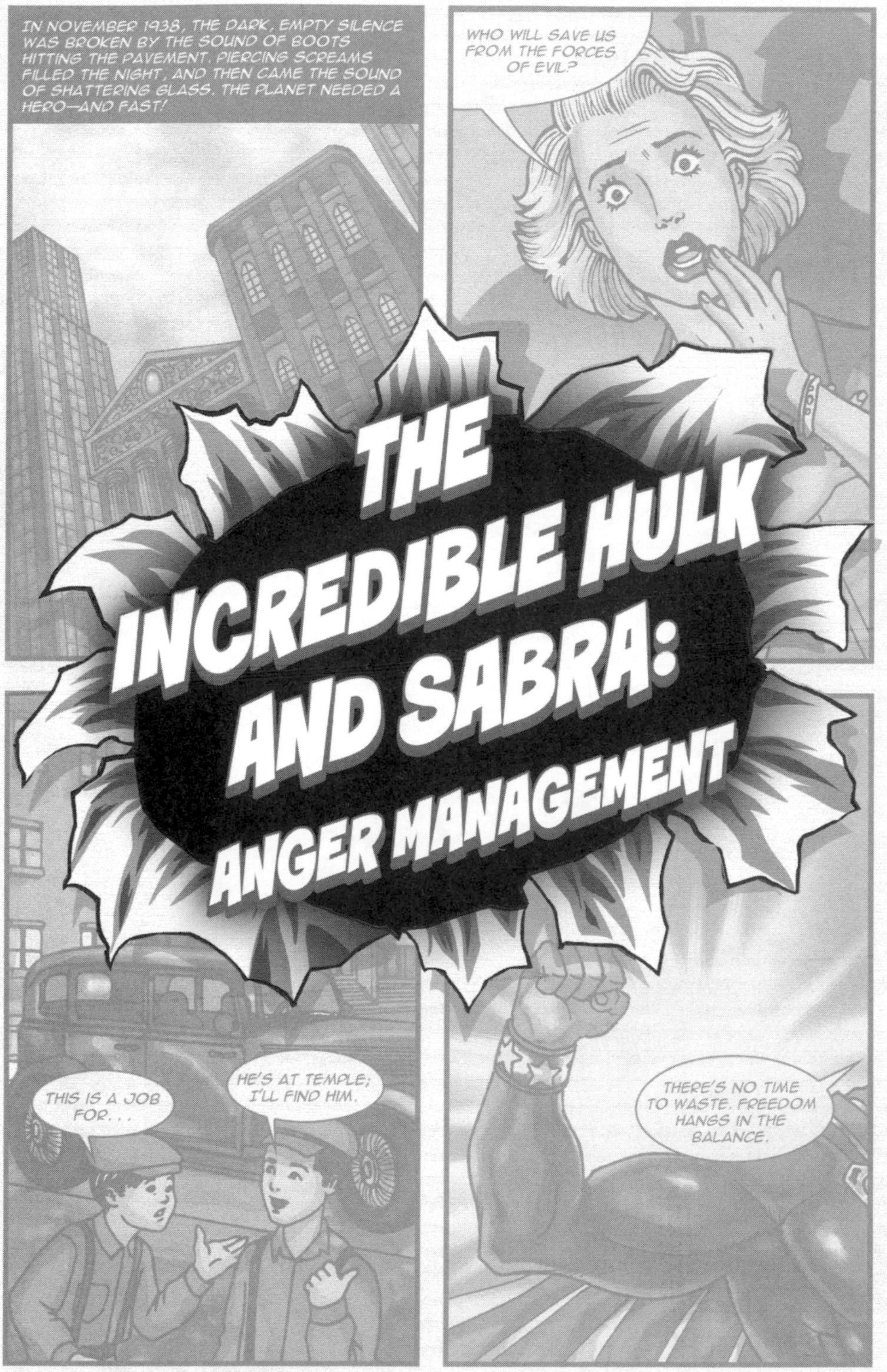

IN NOVEMBER 1938, THE DARK, EMPTY SILENCE WAS BROKEN BY THE SOUND OF BOOTS HITTING THE PAVEMENT. PIERCING SCREAMS FILLED THE NIGHT, AND THEN CAME THE SOUND OF SHATTERING GLASS. THE PLANET NEEDED A HERO—AND FAST!
WHO WILL SAVE US FROM THE FORCES OF EVIL?
THE INCREDIBLE HULK AND SABRA: ANGER MANAGEMENT
THIS IS A JOB FOR. . .
HE'S AT TEMPLE; I'LL FIND HIM.
THERE'S NO TIME TO WASTE. FREEDOM HANGS IN THE BALANCE.

HULK

YEAR OF BIRTH: 1962
ALTER EGO: Robert Bruce Banner
OCCUPATION: Nuclear physicist
FIRST APPEARANCE IN A COMIC BOOK: *The Incredible Hulk* #1 (May 1962)
SUPERPOWERS: Enhanced strength and invulnerability
ORIGIN OF SUPERPOWER: Exposure to gamma radiation
ARCHENEMY: The Leader
BASE OF OPERATIONS: Everywhere, but prefers New Mexico
MEMBERSHIP: Hulkbusters (formerly the Avengers and the Defenders)
CREATED BY: Stan Lee
FIRST DRAWN BY: Jack Kirby

JEWISH CONNECTION:

In *The Incredible Hulk* #387 (November 1991), Hulk finds himself pummeled not only by the furious fists of Israeli superheroine Sabra but by her malevolent mixed metaphors ("I'm small and you're huge . . . but so is Israel small, and we stand up to our enemies! Attack us and we endure! Drop SCUDs on us and we give as good as we get!").

comp. S.S.J.P.R.   ©1996, 1998, 2002, 2006 LP GameCards   18/124

THE HERALD TRIBUNE RECALLED THAT WHEN "HITLER POURED HIS POX OVER EUROPE . . . FILM MONSTERS CRAWLED FOR COVER. THEY KNEW THEY WERE LICKED— THE PUBLIC HAD ENOUGH HORROR WITHOUT HAVING TO SEE MORE." FOLLOWING PEARL HARBOR, HOWEVER, "THE PUBLIC HAD DIFFERENT IDEAS. MAD GHOULS, WOLF MEN AND FRANKENSTEIN MONSTERS BEGAN TO GET MORE MAIL THAN CONTRACT CUTIES."

—David J. Skal, author, lecturer, and filmmaker

"The Thing had proven that monsters could be popular. He was the member of the Fantastic Four who got the most fan mail,"[1] commented Stan Lee, who realized he was onto something with his grumpy yet lovable monster-hero. Lee's encore to the Thing, the *Incredible Hulk*, debuted in May 1962 and pushed the concept of the "superhero with anger issues" even further.

Brilliant Bruce Banner is working on his latest invention, a gamma bomb, when teenager Rick Jones wanders onto the test site. Rushing to save the young man, "Dr. Bruce Banner is bathed in the full force of the mysterious gamma rays! The world seems to stand still, trembling on the brink of infinity, as his ear-splitting scream fills the air."[2]

This horrendous accident saddles Bruce with a volatile, unshakable second personality, the Hulk: a strapping, spinach-colored powerhouse with little patience for the rules of grammar (or much else), who has been wearing the famous same pair of torn yet strangely intact blue trousers for more than forty years now.

Like the Thing, the Hulk possesses enormous physical strength after his exposure to mysterious rays; his overdeveloped leg muscles let him leap up to three miles in one bound, and he can lift up to one hundred tons with relative ease. But the mutation from Banner to Hulk is unstable, triggered by anger, frustration, and other emotions. If the Thing liked to kvetch, the Hulk was a *meshugana*: "Where Doctor Banner had been gentle, the Hulk was a brute! Where Banner had been civilized, the Hulk was a savage! Where Banner was a man, the Hulk was a monster! A monster of super-human strength, due to the gamma rays which coursed thru his mighty frame!"[3] stated *The Incredible Hulk* #2 (1962).

And like the Thing, the Hulk was an involuntary superhero. He served as a stark warning against the dangers of scientific experimentation and as a thinly veiled metaphor for the social climate of the early sixties. The United States and the Soviet Union were still locked in the cold war, in which physical casualties were few but the emotional fallout was palpable. Anxiety about an imminent atomic attack colored everyday life. More than a few Americans built bomb shelters in their backyards, and schoolchildren were drilled to "duck and cover" under their desks in the event of a nuclear explosion—deadly serious exercises in futility. A few months after the Hulk's debut, the Cuban Missile Crisis brought the world to the absolute brink of nuclear war. It was the climax of tensions that had been building up since 1945. In the early issues of the series, the Hulk frequently battled other atomic and genetic mutations with names like Toad Men, General Fang, and the Metal Master.

Initial sales of *The Incredible Hulk* were respectable but not impressive, and Marvel cancelled the series after just six issues. However, the comic showed tremendous (and unprecedented) popularity among college-aged readers. Kirby received a fan letter notifying him that the Hulk had been chosen as a dormitory mascot. The Hulk stayed alive through guest appearances in other comics until he was reinstated as a hero in his own right in April 1968. In the years that followed, the popularity of the "Green Goliath" (Lee's affectionate nickname for his creation) grew enormously. He starred in cartoons, television shows, and a feature film, becoming the definitive pop culture symbol for anger.

To illustrate his latest creation, Lee turned again to his mentor, Jack Kirby. "Jack," Lee told him, "you're going to think I'm crazy, but can you draw a good-looking monster, or at least a sympathetic-looking monster?"[4] Luckily, Kirby was an expert on the monster archetype.

Warming to his theme of the flawed superhero, Lee didn't put the Hulk in a costume—his own green flesh serves as a costume of sorts. Actually, the Hulk's original color was gray. But the printer couldn't keep Lee and Kirby's chosen shade consistent, so they all agreed to switch to the easier-to-manage green from the second issue onward.

The Hulk is a combination of the Thing and Frankenstein's monster, whom Stan Lee viewed as a misunderstood hero: "To me the monster was the good guy. We always saw the mob of idiots with torches chasing Boris Karloff, who played the monster, up and down the hills until he went berserk, remember? He never really wanted to hurt anybody."[5] The Hulk too is burdened by a threatening appearance, but he never hurts anyone intentionally and longs for friendship.

Here one can draw a symbolic parallel with the Jewish people. Although biblical scriptures talk of the Jewish people serving as "a light unto the nations," Jews have often been feared and mistreated. The modern state of Israel has enriched the world in countless ways, making numerous breakthroughs in medical research and technology. Sadly, all too often these contributions to humanity are overlooked, and Israel is viewed instead as the world's pariah.

Dr. Bruce Banner is pursued by the American military, the same men who once employed him to develop the gamma bomb. Led by the stern General Ross, the military devotes its entire arsenal to killing the Hulk. Ross's daughter Betty has feelings for Banner, but Banner's tragic, secret double life renders him unable to return her affection. Just as the Jewish people were forced to wander from place to place to ensure survival, so too the misbegotten Hulk wanders the planet in an elusive search for sanctuary.

A Jewish alter ego of the Hulk can be found in the Golem, Judaism's own monster-hero. *Frankenstein* author Mary Shelley was inspired by the Jewish legend to invent her famous monster, who, like the Hulk and the Golem, is the result of hubristic man-made engineering. While many superheroes bear a superficial resemblance to the Golem, the Hulk truly personifies this mythical being; he is a powerful if extremely unpredictable protector, the result of an experiment gone horribly wrong.

Remember that originally, the Hulk's skin was gray, like clay. The Hebrew word *golem* is used in biblical literature to refer to an unformed substance, especially a lump of clay or earth. Psalms 139:16 uses the word *galmi*, which means "my unshaped form." The word is also used with reference to the earth from which the first primordial man, Adam, was created. Therefore, one could perhaps deduce that we are, in fact, all golems!

Tales of golems actually predate medieval Prague, the city that legend says the golem protected. The Talmud highlights that the great sage Rabba created a golem using the *Sefer Yetzirah* (Book of Formation). Thousands of years before Dolly, the famous cloned sheep, the Talmud recounts the creation of another living mammal: "Rav Hanina and Rav Hoshaya used to convene every Friday and occupy themselves with the 'laws of creation.' They were able to fashion a calf one-third grown, which they ate."[6]

Michael Chabon's novel *The Amazing Adventures of Kavalier and Clay* tells the story of two Jewish comic book pioneers, loosely based on Superman's Siegel and Shuster. In his book, Chabon draws an analogy between the creation of the Golem and the writing of superhero comics: "Every golem in the history of the world, from Rabbi Hanina's delectable goat to the river-clay Frankenstein of Rabbi Judah Loew ben Bezalel, was summoned into existence through language, through murmuring, recital, and kabbalistic chitchat—was literally talked into life. Kavalier and Clay—whose golem was to be formed of black lines and four-color dots of the lithographer—lay down, lit the first of five dozen cigarettes they were to consume that afternoon, and started to talk."[7]

Similarities between the Hulk and the Golem were confirmed in *The Incredible Hulk* #133 and #134, both edited by Stan Lee, who commented in an interview, "When you think about it, The Incredible Hulk is a golem."[8]

In *The Incredible Hulk* #133 (1970), the Hulk flees the American military and travels to the fictitious Eastern European country Morvania. That nation is overrun by an army resembling the Nazis and is ruled by a dictator named Draxon—"where Hitler failed . . . where Napoleon stumbled and fell . . . there shall Draxon succeed."[9] An underground resistance army is led by an obviously Jewish man named Isaac. Bearded and clad in a flat cap, he recalls Teviyah from *Fiddler on the Roof*, the quintessential Jewish character in the minds of many Americans. Isaac's wife is named Rebecca and his daughter Rachel, both the names of Jewish matriarchs. The Hulk is inadvertently drawn into a conflict with Draxon and his army.

In the next issue, #134 (1970), Isaac's young daughter mistakes the Hulk for a golem that has come to save the city. She brings home the Hulk, declaring to her father, "He's the one you told me about! The Golem." Isaac does not share his daughter's fantasy, and once again the Hulk is shunned. However, Isaac soon changes his mind, recalling the Golem of Prague. "Rabbi Judah Low Ben Bezalel breathed life into a body without a soul! Yea, common clay stood upright—a thing of mud and wattle fought with demon-like frenzy . . . until our people were safe . . . then the creature of Rabbi Low vanished . . . turned back into a statue, some said . . . or wandered off to new lands, said others . . . perhaps even here . . . to Morvania!"[10]

Isaac decides that the Hulk could really be their savior. "We must find him, reason with him, persuade him to be our protector, our golem!" Only after Rachel pleads with the Hulk, crying, "Be our golem . . . please . . . help us!" does the Hulk indeed defeat Draxon and his army. Isaac declares, "You were our golem, and we'll have no more kings in Morvania—no more dictators." The story ends as Hulk disappears into the distance mumbling, "Golem! Wonder, what is a golem?"[11]

Unlike the Golem, the Hulk has an alter ego he can change into, Bruce Banner. The notion of dual personalities vying for the same body can be traced back to Robert Louis Stevenson's creation of Dr. Jekyll and Mr. Hyde. This concept of the divided man can also be seen in the work of Sigmund Freud, who believed the human psyche was mercilessly possessed by three constantly vying energies: the id, the ego, and the superego.

Jewish thought has an equivalent concept. According to the Talmud, people are born with two opposing impulses: the *yetzer hatov*, the impulse to do good, and the *yetzer harah*, the impulse to do evil. Jewish sages have noted that the *yetzer harah* is not completely evil but rather can be depicted as the selfish impulse, which needs to be balanced with *the yetzer hatov*, the selfless impulse. Thus, in Jewish thought, everybody, like Banner, battles his or her own personal Hulk.

As in the case of other superheroes, the Hulk's strength recalls that of the biblical Samson. The series contains more obvious references to Samson as well. A character named Doctor Leonard Samson, a psychiatrist who believes he can cure the Hulk, appears in #141 (1971). The nerdy Doctor Samson empowers himself through a controlled dose of radiation and becomes Doc Samson, a massively muscled, green-haired superhuman with gamma-boosted strength sporting long hair like his biblical namesake. Cutting Doc Samson's hair saps his power, too. In #227 (1978), Samson proposes therapy for the Hulk (a particularly Jewish remedy?) and constructs a steel-reinforced psychiatrist's couch. And in #373 (1990), Samson's Jewish roots are confirmed when he admits he attended Yeshiva and that he is intimidated by "a very strict rabbi."[12]

The core of the Hulk's personality is anger, a topic that Judaism deals with at length. In Jewish mystical thought, anger is compared to fire. Like fire, which can consume its surroundings, anger also can consume a person with rage. Maimonides equates anger with idolatry: "One who gets angry is compared to someone who has committed idolatry—an idol worshipper."[13]

Bruce Banner often became enraged, and for good reason. After all, here is a scientist who was destroyed by science. Later editions of the comic portray Bruce's father as a less-than-perfect parent who demonized his son for his high intellect.

The Arizal, a sixteenth-century kabbalist, took the self-imploding dangers of anger so seriously that he taught his students a drastic rectification for anger: 151 days of consecutive fasting! Even in today's diet-crazed society, this seems a little extreme. Therefore, contemporary kabbalists suggest making monetary donations in the denomination of 151 instead. Why 151? Because of the mystical concept of *gematria*. In this complex system, the letters of the Hebrew alphabet are accorded numerical equivalents. According to *gematria*, the number 151 is the numeric computation for the two names of God in the Bible, Elokim and Adonoi. Elokim (the aspect of God within nature) equals 86, and Adonoi (the aspect of God that transcends nature) equals 65; 86 plus 65 equal 151. The numerical computation of the word "anger" (*ka'as* in Hebrew) is 150. Consequently, according to Kabbalah, as a way to transform anger into godliness, we must add the oneness of God to our lives.

Over the course of the comic series, as the Hulk roams the world in search of meaning and acceptance, it seems inevitable that he would eventually reach the place that people throughout history have made pilgrimages to: the Holy Land of Israel. In the 1981 issue #256, entitled "Power and Peril in the Promised Land" (written by Bill Mantlo and illustrated by Sal Buscema, both non-Jewish), the Hulk does just that. "After weeks at sea, the freighter, *Star of David*, returns home."[14] Bruce is a stowaway on the ship, which docks at the seaport of Tel Aviv.

Rudely awakened, he turns into the Hulk. Little does he realize he's about to meet another superhero: his opposite in appearance but one who shares the Hulk's "anger issues."

Patrolling the dock at this time is a young, dark-haired, feisty Israeli policewoman with a secret. "The military are in no shape to go after the

Hulk!" she declares. "That leaves me to stop the monster before he menaces the rest of Tel Aviv!"[15] At that, the policewoman transforms into Sabra, superheroine of the state of Israel. Sabra's costume, like the Israeli flag, is blue and white, emblazoned with a Star of David.

Sabra can't catch the Hulk, who then changes back into Bruce Banner. Later, a terrible tragedy reawakens the Green Goliath. Banner befriends a young Arab boy named Sahad, a cheeky, lovable rogue who runs around barefooted, stealing watermelons and collecting money "for a mother and fifteen sisters." Sahad is killed when a restaurant is bombed. Masked terrorists enter the devastation, shouting, "In the name of Arab sovereignty over these lands, we deal retribution to those who would steal from us!"[16] Enraged, Banner transforms back into the Hulk to take on the terrorists. Sabra flies to the rescue and, mistaking the Hulk for a terrorist, attacks him with her "energy quills." The pair tussle, but there is no clear victor.

Ultimately, Sabra realizes that the Hulk is innocent of any wrongdoing, but he leaves Israel angry and frustrated by his experience: "Hulk came looking for peace—but there is no peace here!" The story ends with Sabra on her knees, contemplating her mistake. "It has taken a monster to awaken her own sense of humanity."[17]

Sabra's appearances in later issues of *The Incredible Hulk*, *X-Men*, and other comics reveal more about her life. She was raised on a special government-run kibbutz, served in the Mossad (the Israeli secret service), and lost a young son named Jacob (a reference to the biblical patriarch) in an Arab terrorist attack on an Israeli school bus.

Sabra's full name, Ruth Bat-Seraph (Hebrew for "Ruth, the daughter of Seraph"), also alludes to Jewish biblical traditions. The book of Ruth recalls the story of a young Moabite woman during the time of the Judges, who married a Jewish man from Bethlehem. After her husband dies, Ruth severs her ties to Moab, converts to Judaism, and returns with her mother-in-law, Naomi, to Bethlehem. Later, Ruth marries a wealthy Bethlehemite named Boaz and becomes the great-grandmother of King David. Jewish tradition praises Ruth's faith and loyalty, making "Ruth" an apt name for a superheroine!

The word "seraph" has dual connotations. It refers to a kind of snake (see Numbers 21:6 and Deuteronomy 8:15). Isaiah 14:29 and 30:6 mention a "flying seraph," an allusion to a mythical species of serpent. Another understanding of the seraph is as a heavenly creature that helps angels and guards the Holy ark. This kind of seraph is mentioned in Isaiah 6:2. These divine creatures with three sets of wings continuously proclaim God's holiness in heaven. Again, the name "Seraph" seems well chosen for a righteous warrior.

"Sabra" is the word used to describe a Jew born in the Holy Land of Israel. The word is derived from the Hebrew *tzabar*, the prickly pear cactus. Rough to the touch, this desert plant has a sweet interior. Israelis may sometimes seem prickly, but this is simply a natural defense mechanism. They are a kind and benevolent people at heart. Not only is Sabra an Israeli sabra, but her weapons resemble her cactus namesake: sharp-pointed energy quills.

The comic book genre boasts few female superheroes. Wonder Woman and Supergirl are exceptions, but they remain overshadowed by their male counterparts. Sabra, however, refuses to stand in anyone's shadow. By taking on the Hulk, she shows her courage as a true superhero and earns a place among the luminaries. While Sabra longs for peace, she recognizes that sometimes action must be taken. Sabra series editor Tom Brevoort commented, "In terms of what we've seen in her chronicled adventures, she's probably more of a hawk than a dove."[18]

Not surprisingly, the character of Sabra boasts a dedicated Jewish following. One online petition campaigns for Sabra to be given a comic of her own "to help bring peace" and calls her "a very cool character."[19]

The reverse of a stereotypical female character, Sabra is physically powerful—and willing to use that power in battle. Saving the world in comics (and in the real world) largely seems to be a male pursuit, but Jewish tradition recounts several stories of heroic females. For example, the book of Judges relates the story of Deborah. God tells Deborah to save the people from twenty years of oppression by King

Jabin of Canaan. Deborah, whose name is an anagram of "she spoke" (*dibrah*), ensures a Jewish victory not by fighting but with her counsel. Deborah leaves the action to Yael, the clan leader's wife and another heroic woman. Sisera, the commander of King Jabin's army, escapes to the Kenite camp after his defeat. Yael invites him to stay in her tent. When he falls asleep, Yael drives a tent peg through his head.

Another story of feminine bravery is read every year during Hanukkah. Yehudis, the daughter of Yochanan Kohen Gadol, saves many Jews by killing the Greek leader Holopurnus. Yehudis feeds Holopurnus cheese and wine until he falls into a deep sleep. Yehudis draws Holopurnus's own sword and decapitates him. Take that, Wonder Woman!

In Judaism, women are accorded a spiritual standing higher than that of men. The Bible describes the creation of the first woman, Eve, using the word *vayiven*, meaning "God built," which shares the same root as the Hebrew *binah*, meaning "insight" or "understanding." The Talmud deduces from this that women were created with greater wisdom and understanding.

Michael Chabon, in an essay entitled "A Woman of Valor" (which he calls an "open love letter disguised as a pseudo-scholarly treatise on super heroines") discusses his frustrations with the typical female superhero. "Wonder Woman's story just never added up." Supergirl, he writes, "was a classic *shikse* as envisioned by Jewish men of the day." Chabon's favorite female superhero is a little-known Jack Kirby creation from 1972 called Big Barda. "Biographers and scholars generally agree, [Big Barda] was modeled on the late Rosalind Kirby (nee Goldberg), Jack's wife of fifty years."[20]

Chabon concludes his essay commenting, "It's traditional in Jewish homes, on the Sabbath, for a husband to chant the poem called *Eshes Chayil*, 'A Woman of Valor.' In ancient biblical language he praises her, articulating a litany of true womanly virtues: strength of body and mind, compassion, resourcefulness, reliability, artfulness. He praises her costume, and her readiness for righteous battle. 'She girds her loins in strength,' is what he says, 'and makes her arms strong.' Every week, in every home—traditionally—every husband affirms this central truth to every wife: that she is, as that great Jewish mythographer Jack Kirby understood, his Big Barda."[21]

Chabon is smart enough to recognize the tough resilience, as well as the grace and beauty, of the Jewish woman—a true superhero by anyone's standards.

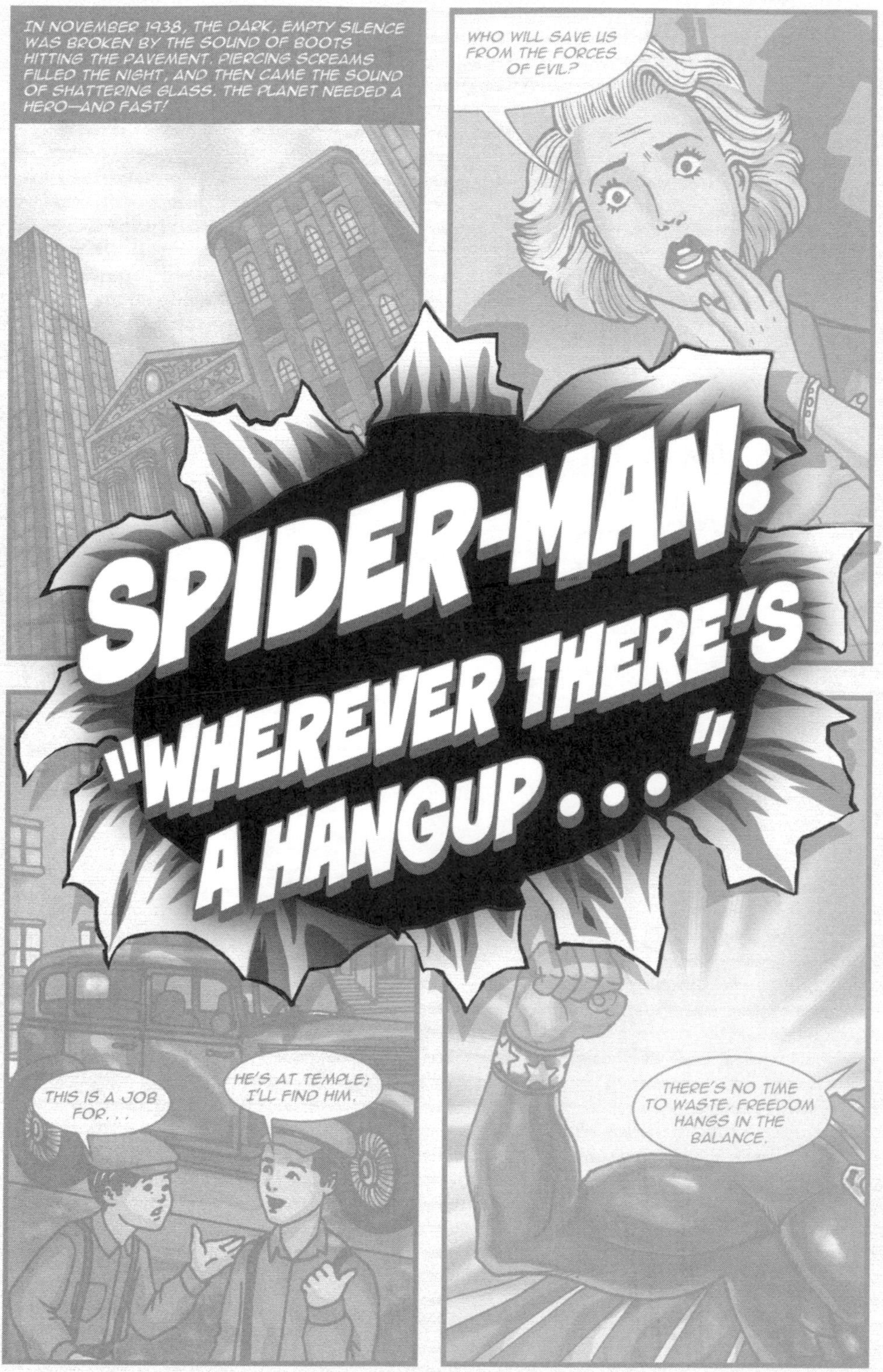
IN NOVEMBER 1938, THE DARK, EMPTY SILENCE WAS BROKEN BY THE SOUND OF BOOTS HITTING THE PAVEMENT. PIERCING SCREAMS FILLED THE NIGHT, AND THEN CAME THE SOUND OF SHATTERING GLASS. THE PLANET NEEDED A HERO—AND FAST!
WHO WILL SAVE US FROM THE FORCES OF EVIL?
SPIDER-MAN: "WHEREVER THERE'S A HANGUP . . ."
THIS IS A JOB FOR. . .
HE'S AT TEMPLE; I'LL FIND HIM.
THERE'S NO TIME TO WASTE. FREEDOM HANGS IN THE BALANCE.

SPIDER-MAN

YEAR OF BIRTH: 1962

ALTER EGO: Peter Benjamin Parker

OCCUPATION: Freelance photographer

FIRST APPEARANCE IN A COMIC BOOK: *Amazing Fantasy* #15 (August 1962)

SUPERPOWERS: Enhanced strength, speed, and agility; ability to sense danger before it occurs with a "spider-sense"; web-shooters that spin artificial webbing from his gloves.

ORIGIN OF SUPERPOWER: Bite from a radioactive spider

ARCHENEMY: Various

BASE OF OPERATIONS: New York

MEMBERSHIP: None

CREATED BY: Stan Lee

FIRST DRAWN BY: Jack Kirby

JEWISH CONNECTION:

In *Web of Spider-Man* #57 (November 1989), Spider-Man battles a racist skinhead who has been transformed into a superpowered blob. The blob, known as Skinhead, was trying to kill Rabbi Chaim Cross—the skinhead's father! (The premise of a young Jewish man becoming a violent racist may seem to be the stuff of comic book fantasies, but the story of a Jew named Daniel Burros who became involved with the Ku Klux Klan and the American Neo-Nazi Party was the basis for the 2001 film *The Believer*.)

REMEMBER, HOLLYWOOD IS RUN BY JEWS. SO, WHEN YOU INTRODUCE YOURSELF AT MEETINGS, IT'S [PRONOUNCED] "SPIDER-MIN." IRVING SPIDERMAN.

—Jon Stewart, host, *The Daily Show*

A band of masked robbers cleans out the vaults of a New York bank and heads for the roof. The thieves jump into a waiting helicopter and make their escape, congratulating each other on their successful heist—"like taking candy from a baby." The chopper swoops between Manhattan skyscrapers at breakneck speed. No one can stop them now.

Suddenly, the helicopter slams to a violent and complete stop, then hurtles backward. In a series of jump cuts, the camera zooms out, farther and farther—until viewers realize the helicopter is actually entangled in a giant spider's web, suspended between the World Trade Center's twin towers. Spider-Man caught those thieves "just like flies," as his 1960s theme song states. That thrilling teaser trailer for Columbia Pictures' *Spider-Man* movie came out in the summer of 2001—and was quickly yanked after the tragic events of September 11. A related poster, showing the World Trade Center reflected in the web slinger's eye, was shelved too.

After September 11, the American people were shell-shocked with grief and fear, but eventually they also yearned to take solace in popular culture. When the eagerly awaited *Spider-Man* movie finally came out in 2002, it smashed all previous box office records. Filmgoers clearly needed a powerful yet lovable hero who would come to New York's rescue, even if it was all just make-believe. Who better than that quintessentially New York superhero, the wisecracking, hyperkinetic (and slightly neurotic) Spider-Man?

In 2002, Spider-Man had been fighting crime and wisecracking for an amazing forty years. In August 1962, Stan Lee was basking in the success of the Fantastic Four and the Hulk. With his passion for comic books renewed, Lee pitched yet another character to Marvel publisher Martin Goodman, a new kind of superhero: "A teenager, with all the problems, hang-ups, and angst of any teenager. He'd be an orphan who lived with his aunt and uncle, a bit of a nerd, a loser in the romantic department, and who constantly worried about the fact that his family had barely enough money to live."[1] In other words, like Lee's other Silver Age characters, Spider-Man isn't a patriotic assimilation fantasy who possesses Superman's or Batman's stoic self-confidence.

The reaction? Goodman hated it. Teenagers were sidekicks, not heroes, he insisted. Everybody knew that. But to keep Lee happy, Goodman stuck Lee's creation on the cover of an anthology title that was getting cancelled anyway. To everyone's surprise, *Amazing Fantasy* #15 (1962) enjoyed a huge spike in sales. Martin's philosophy about adolescent superheroes changed overnight. "Stan, remember that Spider-Man idea of yours that I liked so much? Why don't we turn it into a series?"[2] Lee recalled years later.

The cover for *Amazing Fantasy* #15 had been illustrated by Jack Kirby, but Lee felt that Jack's style was too larger than life to truly capture his vision of a "friendly neighborhood" Spider-Man, so he turned to artist Steve Ditko.

Angst-ridden teenager Peter Parker is introduced in the first panel as "that bookworm [who] wouldn't know a cha-cha from a waltz!"[3] He's drawn as a nebbish—a dark-haired, spectacled, neurotic worrier. When he's bitten by a radioactive spider while visiting a science museum, Peter ends up with an array of superhuman, spider-like powers: speed, strength, and agility; a tingling "spider-sense" that warns him of impending danger; the ability to quickly recover from injuries and poisons; and a proficiency for sticking to walls. Originally nearsighted, Peter now has perfect vision.

While other superheroes use their powers to battle monstrous villains and promote world peace, at first all poor Peter Parker wants to do is make a living. He cooks up a brilliant costume to match his new alter ego—Spider-Man—and becomes an instant wrestling star. Then after one bout, an apathetic Peter lets a robber run past him. The same criminal subsequently murders Peter's beloved Uncle Ben. "My fault, all my fault!" he sobs. "If only I had stopped him when I could have! But I didn't . . . and now my uncle Ben is dead."[4] From then on, driven by the sense of responsibility for his uncle's death, Peter devotes himself to fighting injustice.

The final panel of this first issue depicts Peter in somber silhouette, walking into the distance: "And a lean silent figure slowly fades into the gathering darkness, aware at last that in this world, with great power there must also come . . . great responsibility!"[5]

This immortal line about power and responsibility sounds almost biblical, but Stan Lee insists it was just a throwaway. Lee once said, "It was just a phrase that came to me and it sounded good, and I wrote it down and continued writing without giving it much more thought."[6] Despite Lee's recollection, it is tempting to think that the stirring cadences of President John F. Kennedy's 1961 inaugural address were still ringing in his ear:

In the long history of the world, only a few generations have been granted the role of defending freedom in its hour of maximum danger. I do not shrink from this responsibility—I welcome it. I do not believe that any of us would exchange places with any other people or any other generation. The energy, the faith, the devotion which we bring to this endeavor will light our country and all who serve it—and the glow from that fire can truly light the world. And so, my fellow Americans: ask not what your country can do for you—ask what you can do for your country.[7]

The death of a loved one is a commonplace motive for crime fighting in comics. Just think of Batman. But Spider-Man is driven by guilt rather than revenge. Michael Chabon notes, "I don't think there's another comic-book superhero that's as completely driven by trying to pay some debt, a debt that can't be paid, as Spider-Man is."[8]

Jewish guilt seems to be a largely American phenomenon. In fact, there is no Hebrew word for guilt! Freedom, affluence, and acceptance came only after the Jewish people had suffered to preserve their faith through thousands of years of persecution and near annihilation. Sam Raimi, director of the hugely successful *Spider-Man* movies, agrees with Chabon: "Spider-Man is a character that spends his life trying to pay down his guilt. The only difference is that it's caused by his uncle, not his mother. That's a real classically Jewish quality—to be very aware of your sins in this life and try and make amends for them in this life."[9]

The theme of guilt leads to talk of Spider-Man being Jewish. So does Spider-Man's dry sense of humor. "He's a very funny guy, almost Seinfeld with webbing,"[10] observes Marvel writer Danny Fingeroth. Chabon comments, "For years people have speculated that Peter was sort of crypto-Jewish. You know, living with his uncle Ben and aunt May in Queens."[11] Spider-Man, unlike other superheroes, is more of a Woody Allen nebbish, suffering from stereotypical Jewish neuroses. When in his Clark Kent guise, Superman was only pretending to be a nerd. Peter Parker really was one. As Stan Lee explained, "Most of the young readers could identify with him because he had all the hangups that they did . . . in a story, I'd have his costume tear or he'd get an allergy attack. He'd be worried about acne or dandruff or an ingrown toenail."[12]

Sam Raimi is also a member of the tribe, whose parents are of Russian and Hungarian Jewish descent. Raimi saw in his own *zaddy*

(Yiddish for grandfather) a type of heroism akin to Peter Parker's. "He acted as a sponsor for many Jews that came from Poland before the war closed those borders," Raimi said. "My father is very proud of that and so am I."[13]

Raimi admits to being fascinated by Michael Chabon's fictional account of the early days of the comic book industry, *The Amazing Adventures of Kavalier and Clay.* "You understand how badly the comic creators themselves needed heroes . . . Being from a Jewish family which was destroyed in Poland in the Second World War I really related to that because I knew it was the story of my family too. My grandfather tried to warn his family that the Nazis were coming and they just didn't believe it."[14]

While Spider-Man creator Stan Lee says he did not intend the character to be Jewish, he does hint that he's infused his characters with Jewish ethics. "To me you can wrap all of Judaism up in one sentence, and that is, 'Do not do unto others . . .' All I tried to do in my stories was show that there's some innate goodness in the human condition. And there's always going to be evil; we should always be fighting evil."[15]

"Of all the biblical characters," Lee noted, "I would have to say Spider-Man most resembles David."[16] He pointed out the story of the biblical king's special relationship with the eight-legged creature.

As a young boy, David tried to fathom the meaning behind each animal, but he couldn't figure out the spider. David thought the spiders wove wonderful webs, but otherwise he could see no use for them. When David asks God about it, God replies that one day, David will understand what makes spiders so special.

David grows up and becomes a courageous warrior, defeating the giant Goliath and other enemies of Israel. But his father-in-law, King Saul, is jealous of David's popularity, so he sends his soldiers to kill him. David is forced to hide out in the wilderness, with King Saul's men in hot pursuit. David finds a cave to hide in. As he hears the king's

Spider-man

101

men growing closer, David sees a big spider start spinning a web all the way across the opening of the cave. When the soldiers start to enter the cave, they run into the web. Figuring the presence of the web proves that David couldn't be hiding in the cave, the soldiers march away. So because of the spider, David's life is saved. He praises God for creating all creatures.

◆ • ◆

Many people consider spiders pests and are fearful of them, but in fact these creatures perform a vital natural function by keeping the insect population under control. In the same way, the Jewish people have received their share of bad press over the years. Israel is a special target of misrepresentation in media "spin." Like the Jewish people, Spider-Man tries to do what's right but is viewed with suspicion by authority figures. In fact, he is often considered no better than a lawbreaker himself, thanks largely to a high-profile smear campaign run by wacky J. Jonah Jameson, publisher of the *Daily Bugle*. Ironically, Peter works as a freelance photographer for Jameson, selling photographs of himself as Spider-Man.

Spider-Man's famous costume covers his entire body from head to toe. Even his eyes hide behind unblinking white triangles. Spider-Man seems to be trying particularly hard to conceal himself; not many other comic book characters are so thoroughly disguised. Spider-Man's complete anonymity can be seen as a Jewish quality. For example, tradition states one of the greatest levels of charity (*tzedakah*) occurs when one gives anonymously. Maimonides comments, "The greatest sages used to walk about in secret and put coins into the doors of the poor."[17] The Talmud states, "R. Eleazar said: A man who gives *tzedakah* in secret is greater than Moses our Teacher, for of Moses it is written, 'For I was afraid because of the anger and the wrath,' and of one who gives *tzedakah* [secretly] it is written, 'A gift in secret subdues anger.'"[18] Thus, by acting in secret, superheros like Spider-Man are doing their part to save the world—and themselves.

◆ ● ◆

From Adam's fig leaf to Joseph's coat, clothing plays an important part in the story of the Jewish people. The two Hebrew words for clothing are *beged* and *levush*. The word *beged* has the same Hebrew letters as the word *bagad*, which means "to sin or rebel." Clothing serves as a reminder of the first sin of man. Originally, Adam and Eve were unclothed, but as a consequence of sin, the evil inclination entered their souls and caused them to be embarrassed by their nakedness. Thus, the word *beged* is a reminder of the sin of man and why people now need clothing.

Fittingly, the Talmud (Shabbos 77b) teaches that the word *levush* is an acronym for the words *lo bosh,* translated as "there is no embarrassment." Clothing covers the body and removes embarrassment. In contrast to the word *beged*, *levush* focuses on the physical function of clothing. *Beged* refers to its spiritual character.

While a discussion of Jewish connections to superhero clothing may seem a little strained, a 2004 edition of *The Amazing Spider-Man* ("Do You Want Pants with That?") reveals the unbelievable truth: all superhero costumes are actually designed by a Jewish tailor from the Lower East Side.

Tailor Leo Zelinsky first sees Spider-Man hurtling across the New York skyline. An unimpressed Zelinsky mutters, "*Meshugge.*" When the two meet, he makes insulting remarks about Spider-Man's costume: "The fabric, I'm guessing Spandex, something like that. You overheat a lot in this thing, don't you? You got no weather-proofing, no proper ventilation . . . you could get athlete's foot all over your body in a thing like this."[19]

It turns out he's been the tailor to superheroes and supervillains both—the "supertailor"! Flashbacks reveal Zelinsky fitting the Thing with size 70 pants, sewing Captain America's uniform, repairing Thor's size 56-long tunic, and even repairing Dr. Doom's cloak.

Zelinsky believes minding his own business is good for business. He serves hero and villain alike, not caring what they do after they leave his shop. But after overhearing an assassin's plans to kill a public official, Zelinsky's grandson makes a Holocaust comparison and persuades the old tailor to alert the police. Once again, guilt is the motivator when the grandson remarks, "Your dad used to watch people passing by when he was in the camp in Poland, and he just wanted one of them, any of them, to look at him, to get involved. He said that you said the most cowardly thing a man can do is to not get involved when something wrong is being done to someone."[20]

So Zelinsky turns in the bad guy, the bad guy turns on Zelinsky, and Spider-Man saves the day. Zelinsky's grandson praises both his *zaddy* and Spider-Man's actions, remarking, "Clothes don't make heroes. What makes a hero is what happens in your heart."[21]

The final panel shows Spider-Man looking at a revised costume design drawn by Zelinsky. It comes with a note: "You ever need a look like this, you come see me. I'll give you a good price." It may be the only bargain Spidey gets for a long time. The long-suffering superhero knows very well that responsibility comes at a high price.

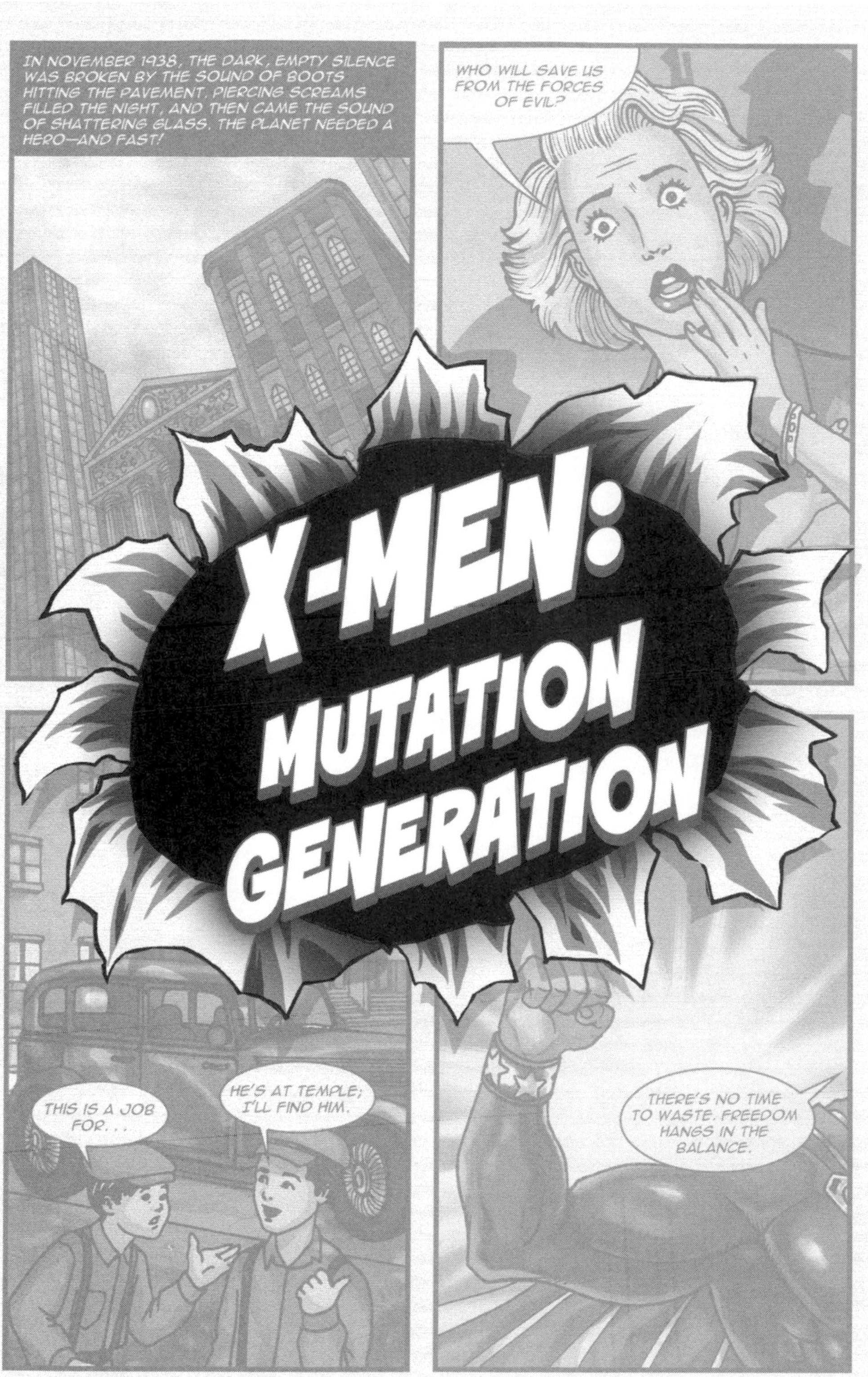
IN NOVEMBER 1938, THE DARK, EMPTY SILENCE WAS BROKEN BY THE SOUND OF BOOTS HITTING THE PAVEMENT. PIERCING SCREAMS FILLED THE NIGHT, AND THEN CAME THE SOUND OF SHATTERING GLASS. THE PLANET NEEDED A HERO—AND FAST!
WHO WILL SAVE US FROM THE FORCES OF EVIL?
X-MEN: MUTATION GENERATION
THIS IS A JOB FOR. . .
HE'S AT TEMPLE; I'LL FIND HIM.
THERE'S NO TIME TO WASTE. FREEDOM HANGS IN THE BALANCE.

MAGNETO

YEAR OF BIRTH: 1963

ALTER EGO: Magnus (real name unknown, alias Erik Magnus Lehnsherr)

OCCUPATION: Revolutionary and conqueror (formerly teacher of the New Mutants, secret agent, and volunteer orderly)

FIRST APPEARANCE IN A COMIC BOOK: *X-Men* #1 (September 1963)

SUPERPOWERS: Absolute control of magnetism

ORIGIN OF SUPERPOWER: Latent mutant ability, which manifested at puberty

ARCHENEMY: The X-Men

BASE OF OPERATIONS: Everywhere (formerly Professor Xavier's School for Gifted Youngsters, an island in the Bermuda Triangle, and Asteroid M)

MEMBERSHIP: None (formerly Acolytes, Hellfire Club, New Mutants, X-Men, and Brotherhood of Evil Mutants)

CREATED BY: Stan Lee

FIRST DRAWN BY: Jack Kirby

JEWISH CONNECTION:

In the *Twisted Toyfare Theatre* story "Seder-Masochism," reprinted in *Twisted Toyfare Theatre* volume 1 (2003), not only does Magneto end his battle with the Fantastic Four abruptly (so as not to fight past sundown on a Friday), he wears a special yarmulke while attending the Thing's Seder. Though it looks like an ordinary yarmulke, it is psychic-proof, thus foiling the attempts of Professor X to overtake his mind during the holiday.

I REMEMBER MY OWN CHILDHOOD . . . THE GAS CHAMBERS AT AUSCHWITZ, THE GUARDS JOKING AS THEY HERDED MY FAMILY TO THEIR DEATH. AS OUR LIVES WERE NOTHING TO THEM, SO HUMAN LIVES BECAME NOTHING TO ME . . . AS A BOY I TURNED MY BACK ON GOD FOREVER.

—*Uncanny X-Men* #150

In retrospect, 1963 marked the true beginning of the sixties. Martin Luther King Jr. delivered his stirring "I Have a Dream" speech to two hundred thousand civil rights protesters in Washington, D.C. Betty Friedan's blockbuster book, *The Feminine Mystique*, unleashed a feminist revolution, while millions of readers learned a new word from Rachel Carson's *The Silent Spring*: "environmentalism." The horrific assassination of President Kennedy and the conspiracy theories that grew up around it shattered America's innocence and peace of mind.

And Stan Lee collaborated again with Jack Kirby on a new story, *The Uncanny X-Men*. Initially a failure, *X-Men* eventually became Marvel's most successful franchise.

The premise is simple: an overabundance of the "X gene" is causing random mutations, spawning a race of superhumans with extraordinary powers. These mutants find themselves treated as outcasts by ordinary humans, who view them with suspicion—sometimes with good reason. This basic plot evolved into an epic of mythic proportions, deeply laden with metaphor and allegory.

"In the main study of an exclusive private school in New York's Westchester County, a strange silent man sits motionless, brooding . . . alone with indescribable thoughts."[1] Thus begins *X-Men* #1 (1963), introducing our hero, Professor Charles Francis Xavier, or Professor X. The telepathic, wheelchair-bound Professor X is the headmaster of the School for Gifted Youngsters, which teaches mutants to develop their strange powers for the good of society.

This haven is a necessity because conventional humans see mutants as threats. It doesn't help matters that a minority of disgruntled mutants has actually threatened to wipe out the human race. As a result, all mutants experience hatred and bigotry, just like other outsiders through the ages.

Stan Lee claimed the motivation for creating his storyline was practical. After all, the genetic mutation device saved him from having to invent a new origin for every single character. But the plot's deeper philosophical underpinnings are hard to ignore.

Unlike other comics, *X-Men* is not the story of a single hero, dynamic duo, or fantastic foursome but the saga of an entire race of extraordinary beings. It's easy to conclude that Kirby and Lee were inspired by the experiences of their own people. From the time of the Babylonian captivity and the destruction of the Temple up to the founding of modern Israel, the Jews have been a wandering people, a nation without a country. For centuries, they have been scattered throughout the world. Like Lee and Kirby's fictional mutants, the Jews were misunderstood and persecuted everywhere they tried to settle and treated as scapegoats.

Following in the tradition of superheroes past, the Professor instructs his X-Men to keep their true identities hidden. In the same way, Lee and Kirby had altered their Jewish-sounding names to gain acceptance within American society. Remember, Kirby was born Jacob Kurtzberg, and Lee's real name was Stanley Martin Lieber. Lee later commented, "Nobody had any respect for comics. Consequently, I changed my name. It's a stupid name."[2] Interestingly, Lee's identification still bears his original surname, which suggests a reluctance to abandon his real identity entirely.

Interestingly, the *X-Men* mutants discover their powers around adolescence, which according to Jewish law is the spiritual beginning of adulthood. To prepare for this auspicious occasion, young Jews attend a bar or bat mitzvah training program to acquire the spiritual readiness to "take on the world." However, unlike those after-school Hebrew classes, Xavier's School for Gifted Youngsters offers a "Danger Room" where teenaged mutants can hone their combat training!

A powerful Jewish subtext that runs throughout the entire *X-Men* series can be detected in the complex villain/antihero named Magneto. He debuted in the very first issue of the series as a mutant with the power to control all magnetism. Professor X evaluates Magneto's outlook, noting, "Not all want to help mankind . . . some hate the human race, and wish to destroy it! Some feel that the mutants should be the real rulers of earth. It is our job to protect mankind . . . from the evil mutants."[3]

Magneto is given credible ideological justifications for his behavior. In *X-Men* #4 (1964) Magneto recounts how he saved a fellow mutant from vengeful human townsfolk. "Have you forgotten that day, not long ago, when I first came to your village in the heart of Europe? Have you forgotten how the superstitious villagers called you a witch because of your mutant powers? It was I who saved you, keeping the maddened crowd back by means of my magnetic power! You must never forget that! Never!!"[4]

The European locale was no coincidence. It's hard to escape the conclusion that Magneto is meant to symbolize Jewish persecution in Nazi-occupied Europe.

Of course, alternative interpretations of Magneto have been suggested. For decades, fans and critics have debated Magneto's symbolic importance and "true" identity. In the 1960s, college students believed the conflict between the pacifist Professor X and the militant Magneto was an allegorical reference to the philosophical differences between Martin Luther King and Malcolm X. Professor X preaches tolerance and coexistence. Antimutantism exists, he says, but humans are inherently good.

Another interpretation sees Magneto as reflective of the more militant, muscular Jewish self-image that emerged after the Yom Kippur War and the daring raid on Entebbe, except that Magneto is a perversion of this self-image, twisted to the extreme.

In 1966, Lee and Kirby turned over the writing and illustrating of *X-Men* to others. It was Jewish writer Chris Claremont who gave the original characters their complex personalities and backgrounds and developed the backstory that confirms the Jewish link to the X-Men. "I was trying to figure out what was the most transfiguring event of our century that would tie in the super-concept of The X-Men as persecuted outcasts," remembered Claremont. "It had to be the Holocaust!"[5]

In perhaps the most poignant story ever to be introduced to a mainstream comic, Claremont added an extra dimension of emotion, which echoed *Maus*, Art Spiegelman's groundbreaking graphic novel about his father's Holocaust experiences. Claremont explained, "Once I found a point of departure for Magneto, all the rest fell into place, because it allowed me to turn him into a tragic figure who wants to save his People. All that had happened to him defined Magneto. So I could start from the premise that he was a good and decent man at heart. I then had the opportunity, over the course of 200 issues, to attempt to redeem him, to see if he could start over, if he could evolve in the way that Menachem Begin had evolved from a guy that the British considered 'Shoot on sight' in 1945 . . . to a statesman who won the Nobel Peace Prize in 1976."[6]

In *Classic X-Men* #19 (1978, 1988), Magneto first mentions his Holocaust experiences: "I endured one death camp . . . in Auschwitz . . . I will not see another people fear what they do not understand and destroy what they fear."[7] Magneto was always tortured by the fact that he could have stopped the Nazis in Auschwitz if only he had been aware of his incredible powers. What it feels like to be different, to be Jewish, Claremont explained, "became my window through which I could present the *X-Men* Universe to a broader audience."[8]

Magneto stayed alive by working as a member of the Sonderkommando for the Nazis. He was handy with metals (not surprisingly), spoke fluent German, stayed on his masters' good side—and helped the death factory kill thousands of his people, including members of his own family. This only adds to his guilt, shame, and confusion and makes him a more sympathetic, and tragic, antagonist.

Reflecting on his own time spent talking to Holocaust survivors at a kibbutz, Claremont cleverly crafted a backstory depicting Magneto and Professor X as strong allies. Professor X is sent to Israel at the request of Dr. Shomron, an Israeli psychiatrist, to assist in the treatment of a Holocaust survivor named Gabrielle Heller, who is in a coma. Professor X uses his psychic abilities to help her recover. During this time, Magneto is working for the same hospital in Israel, alleviating the distress of fellow survivors. For a brief time, the two men are on the same side, a notion that adds considerable depth and poignancy to the X-Men mythos.

Professor X and Magneto's paradoxical world-views personify contrasting Jewish responses to the Holocaust. Professor X's ideology is dovish, striving for peace and reconciliation, while Magneto is hawkish, embodying the "never again" mantra and striking back.

In *X-Men* vol. 2, #1 (1991), Magneto says, "All my life, I have seen people slaughtered wholesale for no more reason than the deity they worshipped or the color of their skin . . . or the presence in their DNA of an extra, special gene. I cannot change the world but I can . . . and will . . . ensure that my race will never again suffer for its fear and prejudice."[9] Here Magneto makes it clear that "never again" is his philosophy.

Does the Bible have a precedent for Magneto's thirst for vengeance? In one story, Dina, the daughter of Jacob, is raped by the son of the King of Sh'chem. Two of Jacob's sons, Shimon and Levi, trick the men of the town into circumcising themselves. Weakened by the pain of circumcision, the menfolk are no match for the brothers, who kill them all to avenge their sister. But Jacob criticizes his sons' zeal. He says the brothers were wrong to take out their frustrations on the entire town.

The late Simon Wiesenthal, in *Justice, Not Vengeance*, wrote, "Hitler not only murdered millions of Jews and millions of his adversaries, he also morally destroyed millions of Germans and millions of Austrians—what's more, for generations to come." In addition to the civil and criminal prosecution of war criminals, Wiesenthal recommended a "constant coming to terms with the past, and learning from it."[10] There can be no peace without justice, in his view, no justice without honor, no honor without memory.

Sadly, Magneto no longer cares about justice, honor, or peace, only constant preemptive vengeance. He did want justice once upon a time. Before he became the costumed Magneto, he was a double agent for Mossad—hunting Nazi war criminals for the CIA but then secretly turning them over to Israel for trial. This is shown in *Classic X-Men* #19 (1988), in which Claremont deliberately contrasted this moment in Magneto's past with what the character would later become. When the CIA finds out what Magneto is doing, his controller and fellow agents murder Magneto's girlfriend and then try to kill him. Using his mutant powers, Magneto kills the agents and declares himself the enemy of human beings. He swears to forever identify himself as a mutant and not a mere human.

Magneto believes humans want only to imprison and kill mutants (as his Jewish people were destroyed in the Holocaust), so the only way to prevent this genocide is to take power away from humans and control them. But Magneto has not completely forgotten his younger, more idealist days, when he tried to establish a homeland where mutants could live in peace. This safe and sovereign place, called Genosha, is a clear parallel to modern Israel. Tragically, that dream was destroyed when giant robots attacked the island, killing millions of the mutants.

The Holocaust parallel can be seen in other issues. In 1980, Claremont wrote "Days of Future Past," in which mutants are rounded up and put in camps throughout the United States, just as the Nazis rounded up the Jews. Then, in 1982, he wrote "God Loves, Man Kills," which deals with a religious crusade against mutants by Reverend William Stryker, who lobbies Congress to pass a Mutant Registration Act. The act is a clear parallel to the Nuremberg Laws that forced German Jews to wear yellow badges.

Another Jewish connection that Claremont brought to the series was the character of a young Jewish woman, Kitty Pryde. Katherine ("Kitty") Pryde, a Jewish girl from Chicago with the power to phase through solid objects, joined the X-Men in the January 1980 issue. Her paternal grandfather, Samuel Prydeman, was a European Jew, known to have been held in a Nazi concentration camp during World War II. His married sister, Chava Rosanoff, is reported to have died during the Holocaust.

Unlike the Thing, Kitty shows pride (pun intended) in her religion. In one captivating episode, she defeats a vampire not with garlic but rather with her silver Magen David (Shield of David) necklace (*Uncanny X-Men* #159, 1982). In a later issue (*Uncanny X-Men* #199, 1985), Kitty attends the National Holocaust Memorial in Washington, D. C., where she speaks in honor of her grandparents.

Having experienced man's inhumanity to man, Kitty is able to empathize with other minorities. In "Unto Others" (*Marvel Holiday Special*, 1996), she consoles Anita Foster, a black girl whose church has been torched by a racist. Kitty compares the destruction of the church to the desecration of the Jews' Temple two thousand years ago by the Syrian Greeks.

In *Unlimited X-Men* #38 (2002), Kitty Pryde can be found lighting a *yahrtzeit* (remembrance) candle to mark the one-year anniversary of the death of her fellow mutant and sometime boyfriend, Colossus. The anniversary of the death of a loved one is commemorated by lighting a *yahrtzeit* candle, which burns throughout the twenty-four-hour anniversary. The flame of the candle is a potent symbol of the flame of life that once burned brightly and illumined the lives of loved ones who mourn the loss. As Kitty lights the candle, she imagines all the people who have been taken from her life.

Perhaps it is the *yahrtzeit* that provides the most poignant metaphor for the X-Men themselves. Fire possesses dual powers of destruction and illumination. Like the powers of the mutants, fire can be used for good or evil and viewed with admiration or terror. In a world where hatred and bigotry are everyday occurrences, the X-Men challenge readers to empathize with misunderstood minorities rather than condemn them out of fear.

By the summer of 2000, this message reached movie theaters across the world with the film *X-Men*. The movie was a smash hit and spawned a 2003 sequel. Both movies were directed by Bryan Singer, who explained his affinity to the minority X-Men: "My parents are both Jewish. They're of Polish and Russian descent. We observed [high holy days]; it was part of an identity and, of course, anxiety as a kid because we didn't get to have a Christmas tree and presents, which is always the Jewish kid's big complaint."[11]

Summer of 2006 saw the release of the third *X-Men* movie. Jewish director Brett Ratner oversaw the new film. The movie's producer, Avi Arad, has his own thoughtful opinions on the Magneto debate: "I would look, ideologically, more to Jabotinsky and Begin than to Ben-Gurion. Magneto to me is not a villain. But he becomes more like Kahane the more frustrated he is with the way the world is approaching the ones who are different."[12]

These movies introduced the X-Men to a brand-new generation of fans. In a world where a shocking number of people claim never to have heard of the Auschwitz concentration camp,[13] this can only have a positive effect.

Jewish Mutants Discovered?

In an amazing case of art imitating life, the genetic muta-tion of the X-Men has a true-life counterpart in the tribe of the Cohanim (plural of Cohen). The Cohanim, the priestly family of the Jewish people, are believed to be the direct descendents of Aaron, the brother of Moses. If the Cohanim were the descen-dents of one man, could they have a uniform genetic marker? This was the hypothesis of a 1996 scientific study. Noting that the genetic information on the male Y chromosome is practi-cally the same as that of previous generations, the Y chromo-some markers of Cohanim and non-Cohanim were analyzed. A particular marker, named the Cohen Modal Haplotype (CMH), was detected in 98.5 percent of the Cohanim. The chances of these results occurring randomly were less than one in ten thousand. Furthermore, the researchers calculated that the estimated date of the original genetic mutation was 106 gen-erations ago—the exact time that Aaron was born, according to the Bible. [14]

CONCLUSION: SPIRITUAL METAPHORS IN SPANDEX

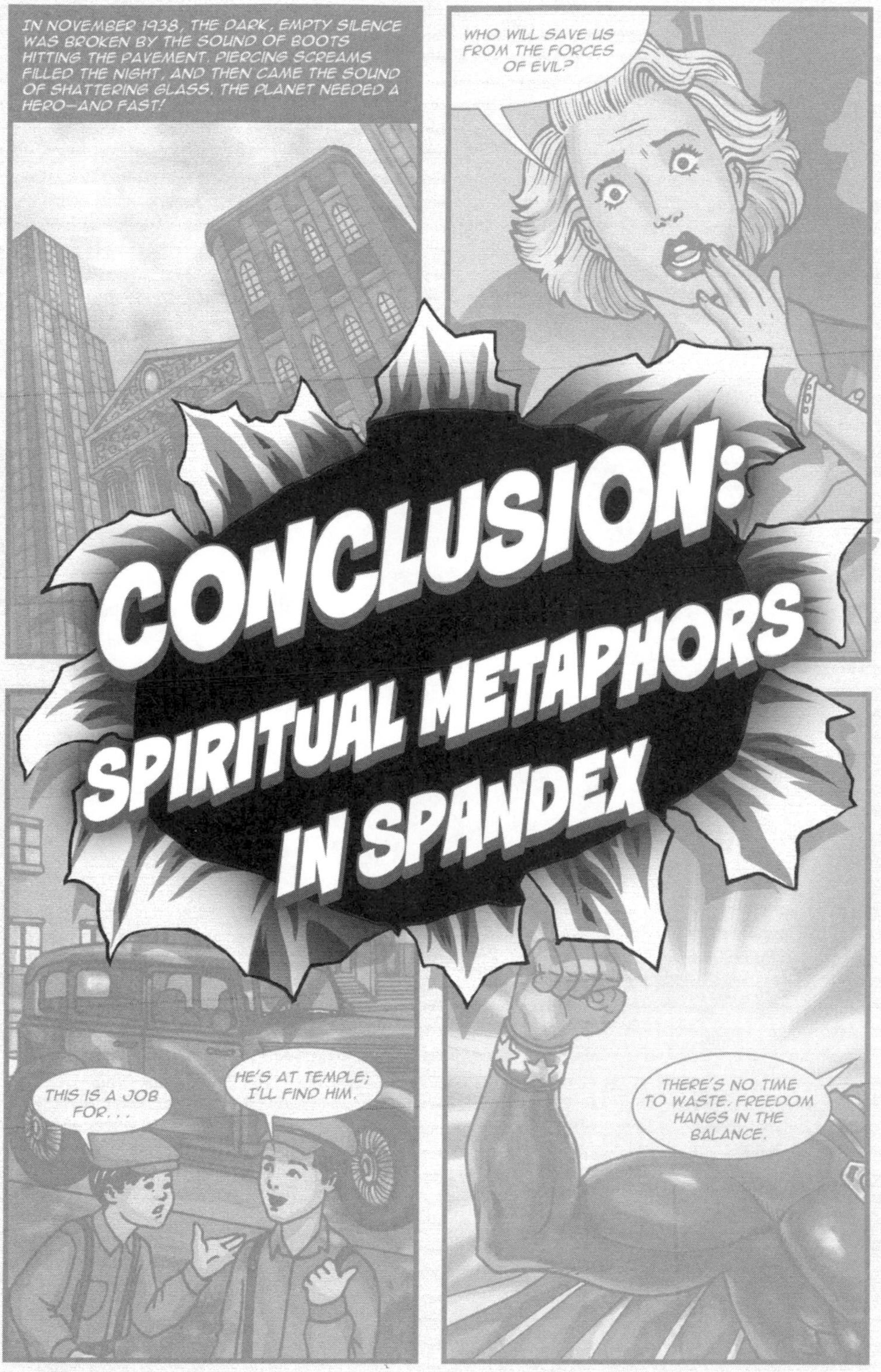
IN NOVEMBER 1938, THE DARK, EMPTY SILENCE WAS BROKEN BY THE SOUND OF BOOTS HITTING THE PAVEMENT. PIERCING SCREAMS FILLED THE NIGHT, AND THEN CAME THE SOUND OF SHATTERING GLASS. THE PLANET NEEDED A HERO—AND FAST!
WHO WILL SAVE US FROM THE FORCES OF EVIL?
THIS IS A JOB FOR. . .
HE'S AT TEMPLE; I'LL FIND HIM.
THERE'S NO TIME TO WASTE. FREEDOM HANGS IN THE BALANCE.

WHEN MEN ARE GROWING UP READING ABOUT BATMAN, SUPERMAN, SPIDERMAN THESE AREN'T FANTASIES, THESE ARE OPTIONS. YOU EVER SEE A GUY MOVING A MATTRESS TIED TO THE ROOF OF HIS CAR. HE'S ALWAYS GOT HIS ARM OUT THE WINDOW HOLDING THIS MATTRESS. THIS IS CLASSIC MALE SUPERHERO IDIOT THINKING. THIS MORON ACTUALLY BELIEVES THAT IF THE WIND CATCHES THE MATTRESS AT 70 MILES AN HOUR—"I GOT IT, I GOT IT. DON'T WORRY, I'M USING MY ARM!"

—Jerry Seinfeld, comedian

Throughout the course of this book, we've watched comic book superheroes evolve to reflect the changing times, as well as the changing attitudes of writers, artists, and readers. In the 1940s, superheroes appointed themselves saviors of a world riddled with real-life villains; their fictional exploits boosted the morale of those fighting flesh-and-blood Nazis, Communists, and other threats to "truth, justice, and the American way." During the tumultuous 1960s, comic book characters became more complex and ambiguous: flawed, reluctant heroes with their own insecurities to cope with (when they weren't fighting crime). Today, in a post-9/11 world that features nothing less than a global conflict of epic proportions, movies such as *Batman Begins* and the *Spider-Man* and *X-Men* series are enormously successful. In 2006, *Superman* returned to the big screen, and not a moment too soon. The world needs him today more than ever.

A phenomenon that deserves a book of its own (stay tuned for *Up, Up, and Oy Vey Part II*?) is the emergence of the graphic novel, a genre that was pioneered in the 1970s by some of the same men who created our original superheroes. These extremely popular comics for adults are more realistic and downbeat—more "artistic." Will Eisner—the comic book pioneer who invented the Spirit and is widely considered the father of the graphic novel—was the first to use the new medium to explore his Jewish heritage and the immigrant experience in America. Like many Golden Age artists and writers, Eisner had used the comic book genre to work out his personal struggles, but in a creative leap he abandoned the old superhero formula for something more naturalistic. The result was his groundbreaking 1978 comic, *A Contract with God*.

Today's Jewish graphic novelists are not afraid to push the boundaries of art and explore their heritage in their work. Unlike their predecessors, they don't have to allude to their backgrounds through allegory or change their names to be successful. Art Speigelman is part of the comic book "underground," an alternative publishing world with plenty of attitude. Spiegelman shot to fame in 1992 when his innovative *Maus: A Survivor's Tale* was awarded a special Pulitzer Prize. Another very different artist addresses the theme of the Holocaust in his own way. Joe Kubert was a Golden Age legend, only eleven years old when he started in the comic book industry back in 1938. He became famous for his work on characters such as Sgt. Rock, Hawkman, and Tor. Like Will Eisner, Kubert eventually switched his focus from superheroes to realism while remaining in the comic book medium. In the early 1990s, Kubert visited the Holocaust Memorial Museum in Washington, D.C., an experience that moved him more than he'd expected. Five years later, his graphic novel *Yossel: April 19, 1943* was published.

These are just a few of the graphic novels that explore Jewish themes. Other Jewish graphic novelists include Harvey Pekar (*American Splendor*), Ben Katchor (*The Jew of New York*), Daniel Clowes (*Ghostworld*), Neil Gaiman (*Sandman*), Joann Sfar (*The Rabbi's Cat*), and Aline Kominsky-Crumb (who collaborates with her husband, underground comics legend Robert Crumb). In the hands of these writers, the superheroes took off their masks and found they didn't need them after all.

With the birth of the graphic novel and the reemergence of the classic superheroes as wildly popular figures in our popular culture, we see how Jewish themes and motifs have boldly found their way to the surface of storylines and character identities. With the passage of time, as Jews became fully integrated into society, the people behind the superheroes became more comfortable with openly expressing their Jewish identity, culture, and values.

In the course of getting to know our favorite superheroes, we've looked at the concerns and issues faced by different generations of Jewish artists and writers and how they grappled with them in the context of their work. Assimilation posed a particularly vexing paradox for mid-twentieth-century American Jews, including those who were creating the likes of the Man of Steel and the Caped Crusader: Can "outsiders" ever really fit in, or must Jews forever straddle two worlds?

For me, as a die-hard superhero fan and as a serious student of the genre, the whole notion of being a Jew behind the mask resonates deeply. When I step back and look at the transition from the Golden Age of comics to the graphic novel, I see myself. I see a young boy named Simon (Simcha is my Hebrew name) who literally spent hours in the bathtub with Star Wars figures creating elaborate new storylines that he imagined would one day fill the big screen. I see an adolescent who today would probably be diagnosed as having obsessive comic book disorder. I see a wide-eyed teenager who was enthralled with the idea of capturing the attention of an audience and inspiring them. I see a film major at Manchester Metropolitan University immersed in pursuing a lifelong dream while desperately trying to avoid an identity he saw as more of a burden than anything else. And then I see myself again, this time as a young man who was beginning to live his dream. I was doing lots of location management for feature films and television dramas set in the north of England. I was going to the parties I had heard so much about and was meeting the producers, directors, and actors I once dreamt of meeting. I still had a long way to go to achieve what I was aiming for, but at last I was walking in the land of the heroes—my heroes.

While I was wielding my nascent powers—the power to decide which crew worked at which location and how sets were to be managed—I began to dabble in exploring my Jewish identity. Something long buried deep inside me was beginning to poke its way to the surface. I began to read a little. I attended a few classes, and I met people who invited me to experience a traditional Shabbat dinner (similar to the one Superman was invited to in *Action Comics* #835, March 2006). I was concurrently meeting my heroes in the film industry and the heroes of my heritage, and the more I got to know my heritage, the more I felt I was getting to know myself. I began to let the mask slip off. Suddenly, the people around me were seeing a whole other side of Simon. But who, alas, was the real Simon Weinstein? The answer to that question came in the form of a television commercial. I was the location manager on a shoot with David Beckham, the larger-than-life megastar of British football. Somehow word got out that Beckham was on the set, and soon the paparazzi were swarming. The shoot was abruptly cancelled and then rescheduled for Saturday, the day I had begun to relate to as Shabbat—the Jewish Sabbath. I tried to think of all the ways I could still do the shoot without compromising the spiritual serenity of Shabbat (I really, really wanted to do that shoot with Beckham), and then finally I said no. I said no to myself, no to my crew, and no to my boss, and I told them why. I told them it was Shabbat and that I was unavailable. The mask was off.

Today, writing this book after years of plumbing the depths of my spiritual heritage, it is clear to me that the comic book superhero has served—both overtly and covertly—as a vehicle for giving a voice to Jewish struggles and Jewish ideas. Does this mean there is a Hebrew school teacher hiding behind the mask of Captain America or Spider-Man?

Hardly. But it does mean that some very genuine Jewish ideas lie within the fantasy worlds of superpeople in colorful tights. I'd like to share a few of these ideas with you.

Let's consider the ubiquitous mask. Like superheroes, every one of us wears a mask, albeit an invisible one. We all wear socially acceptable garb of one kind or another. How many of us put on a brave face for work each morning? How many of us change our appearance in one way or another to try to fit in? This notion of costumes and masks also reflects religious and mystical themes that Jewish comic book creators (not to mention many of their readers) probably took for granted. Not only is the image of the mask prominent in Judaism, but it also embodies some of Judaism's most profound concepts.

The holiday of Purim is a striking example. The story of Purim is told in the book of Esther. Like a superhero, Esther is compelled to hide her true identity. She even had an additional name, Hadassah, which is the Hebrew word for "myrtle." The sages of the Talmud note that Esther, like the myrtle, was "green." Was she a biblical predecessor of the Green Lantern or the Hulk? Not likely. Nonetheless, this duality speaks to Esther's double identity: her ordinary "Clark Kent" side and her heroic "Superman" side. In fact, the Hebrew word *esther* means "hidden." Additionally, the Hebrew term for "book of Esther" is *Megillat Esther*. While *esther* means "hidden," *megillat* means "to reveal." Only the revelation of Esther's true identity enabled her to eventually save the day. It is also striking that the book of Esther is the only book in the Bible in which God's name never appears; his presence remains hidden behind a veil of uncanny events. Eventually, both Esther's true identity and God's behind-the-scenes hand in events is clear for all to see. Both had been hidden in plain sight.

This notion of simultaneous concealed and revealed identities is a recurrent theme in the realm of Jewish mystical thought. The human face is a prime example. The sages teach that every human being has two dimensions: the *chitzoni*, or external dimension, and the *p'nimi*, or inner dimension. Part of us is revealed, and part of us is concealed. The Hebrew word for "face" is *panim*, which means "internal." In Judaism, the face is understood to be a kind of revealed veneer and portal to one's innermost essence. The *p'nimi* is the soul. It's who we are in the deepest sense; it's the source of our most profound aspirations and our ultimate potential. Tradition teaches that the reason no two faces are alike is because on a deeper level—on the soul level—no two people are alike.

Before we take leave of our superheroes, let's take one last look at four of the many spiritual lessons gleaned from our friends in spandex.

1. *In the end, good will prevail.* Ultimately, the superheroes prevail and good triumphs over evil. It's true that along the way, great pain and destruction may be unleashed on Metropolis, but in the end, when the dust clears, evil will have been vanquished.

For thousands of years, no matter where Jews were scattered, no matter how heavy the hand of persecution was, and regardless of which empire happened to rule the land of Israel, the phrase "next year in Jerusalem" was always an integral part of Jewish life and consciousness. The belief in not just a better future but also a remarkably brighter future is the bedrock of Jewish thought. It's no wonder, then, that on Rosh Hashanah (the Jewish new year), a recurrent theme in the holiday prayers is envisioning a time in which good and righteous people will look at the world and "They will see and rejoice . . . and all corruption will disappear like a puff of smoke, and evil rulers will vanish."

No matter how dark the world becomes, no matter how ascendant evil and corruption seem to be, the Jewish belief in the triumph of good over evil and of light over darkness is as unshakable as, well, Captain America himself.

2. *Average people have mighty potential.* No one knows better than Spider-Man: "With great power comes great responsibility." Spider-Man got his superpowers from a spider bite, and with those powers came the responsibility to use them in a just and moral fashion. The sages in the Talmud teach, "Who is mighty? The one who can

conquer his worst inclinations." From the perspective of the sages, each of us was endowed with great "might," and each of us has the responsibility to call upon that mighty power to overcome our worst urges and inclinations.

You and I may not have to confront the likes of the Red Skull or Lex Luthor, but we do have a nemesis of our own. There is a part of us that would like to relax in front of the television rather than get to know our own children or visit a lonely neighbor or parent. There is a part of us that would prefer to sigh and shake our heads when we see human suffering rather than make an effort to alleviate it. There is a part of us that would sooner indulge and titillate our senses rather than master and even elevate them. There is a part of us that would like to ignore our problems rather than confront them. It is precisely in those moments of inner struggle, of tension between doing what is easy and comfortable and doing what is demanding and challenging, that we can discover the horizon of our potential. In the real world, in our day in and day out lives, great responsibility begins with unleashing our own great inner power—the power to do what is right, moral, just, and good—and not just be governed by what tastes, looks, or feels good.

3. *It is never too late.* Many years after robbing a pawnshop, the Thing finally made amends. No matter what else the Thing had done in his life, deep down was an unresolved issue that gnawed away at him, and he had to take care of it.

The Hebrew word for this process of confronting mistakes and making amends is *teshuva,* which literally means "to return." Though time moves in only one direction, spirituality and the soul do not. Judaism has a profound belief in people's ability to go back to a point of departure in life—a point where a serious mistake was made—and to do something about it. We can apologize and repay debts, even after many years. We can look at how we did something wrong or even immoral, return to the moment of decision—revisit, rethink, and reconsider our fateful decision—and then regret the mistake we made and start again. On the deepest level, *teshuva* is about returning to our core of spirituality. There are times, sometimes long stretches of time, when we empower our passions and emotions at the expense of our soul's better judgment. *Teshuva* is the re-empowerment of the soul as the driving force in our lives. It's putting spirituality back in the driver's seat.

4. *You can run, but you cannot hide—from yourself.* Superheroes often feel a desperate urge to conform and to escape the reality of their lives, but that tactic never works. The same is true with us. Sometimes we want to conform, to hide, or to run away from something we sense deep inside ourselves. Often we try to be like others instead of being ourselves. One of my favorite Chassidic stories is about the holy Reb Zushya of Hanipol. Reb Zushya once said to his students, "When I get to heaven, they will not ask me, 'Zushya, why weren't you as wise as Abraham or as great as Moses?' Instead they will ask me, 'Zushya, why weren't you Zushya?'"

What Reb Zushya was telling us is that we are called to be ourselves, not a facsimile of someone else, no matter how super that someone else may be. When all is said and done, the issue is not whether we mimic a hero but whether we unleash the heroic power within ourselves.

◆ ● ◆

I will leave you with a final observation and a request.

Look closely: we are all living in the presence of superheroes. I am privileged to hold several positions of leadership within the Jewish community, and in each setting I encounter remarkable people. As the chaplain of Long Island College Hospital, where I see people in terrible pain, I am regularly awed and humbled by the superhuman efforts of the healthcare professionals who take such fine care of their patients. Besides those efforts, and perhaps because of them, I have witnessed numerous miraculous events. I am also the rabbi of the Pratt Institute, and there—at the very art school that Jack Kirby was too poor to attend—I teach a weekly "Sushi and Kabbalah" class. At Pratt, I see a generation of aspiring Jewish artists who openly grapple with and embrace their faith. I see young people who look at their spiritual lives and say, "As important as school and a career are to me, my faith is at least as important." If they need to work a little harder because they choose not to work on a holiday, they are prepared to make that effort. And then there are the men of Engine Company 224 at the firehouse in the Brooklyn neighborhood where I live. Each one of them selflessly put his life on the line on 9/11 (and many other days too), and each, to me, is a hero. So look around and see if you don't see what I see: real heroes, even superheroes.

So after you put this book down, I ask you to stop and reflect on the real you—the unassailable, essential you. As you go out into the world, go out without any masks and with an embrace of all your unique inner powers. Touch the lives of others, ennoble the lives of others, transform the lives of others, and, better yet, transform the world. Be super—in spandex or not.

Notes

Introduction

1. "Nicholas Cage Sells His Million Dollar Comic Collection," *Southeastern Antiquing and Collecting Magazine*, October 2002, http://www.go-star .com/antiquing/cage.htm.
2. Gene Yang, "History of Comics in Education," http://www.geneyang .com/comicsedu/history.html.
3. National Association of Comic Art Educators, "Teaching Resources," http://www.teachingcomics.org /links.php.
4. Quoted in Michael Weiss, "Secret Identities: The Real-Life Faces behind the Masks of Comic Books' Greatest Super-Heroes," http://www.hoboes .com/pub/Comics/About%20Comics/Essays/Secret%20Identities.

Chapter 1. Superman: From Cleveland to Krypton

1. Quoted in Arie Kaplan, "How Jews Created the Comic Book Industry, Part I: The Golden Age (1933–1955)," *Reform Judaism*, Fall 2003.
2. Jerry Siegel, "Happy Anniversary Superman," Superman.ws: The Superman Website, http://theages.superman.ws/siegel.php.
3. Jerry Siegel and Joe Shuster, "Superman," *Action Comics* #1 (June 1938), reprinted in *Superman: The Action Comic Archives*, vol. 1 (New York: DC Comics, 1997), 16.
4. Siegel, "Happy Anniversary Superman."
5. Harry Brod, "Did You Know Superman Is Jewish?" *Tattoo Jew*, http:// web.archive.org/web/20010411074229/http://www.tattoojew.com/ supermensch.html.
6. Jerry Siegel and Joe Shuster, *Superman* #10 (May–June 1941), reprinted in *Superman: Archives*, vol. 3 (New York: DC Comics, 1991), 125.
7. "Jerry Siegel Attacks!" *Das Schwarze Korps*, April 25, 1940, translated at Randall Bytwerk, "The SS and Superman", German Propaganda Archive, http://www.calvin.edu/academic/cas/gpa/superman.htm.
8. Jerry Siegel and Joe Shuster, *Superman* #1 (Summer 1939), reprinted in *Superman: Archives*, vol. 1 (New York: DC Comics, 1989), 9.
9. Exod. 3:10.
10. Jerry Siegel and Joe Shuster, *Action Comics* #7 (December 1938), reprinted in *Superman: The Action Comic Archives*, vol. 1 (New York: DC Comics, 1997), 28.
11. Judg. 16:28.
12. Jerry Siegel and Joe Shuster, *Superman* #2 (Fall 1939), reprinted in *Superman: Archives*, vol. 1 (New York: DC Comics, 1989), 95.
13. Ibid., 114.
14. *Ethics of the Fathers* 1:18.
15. *Ethics of the Fathers* 5:20.
16. Howard Jacobson, "Is Superman Jewish?" BBC Radio 4, March 5, 2005.
17. Quoted in Brod, "Did You Know Superman Is Jewish?"
18. Jules Feiffer, "The Minsk Theory of Krypton," *New York Times*, December 29, 1996.

19. Jon Bogdanove and Louise Simonson, *Superman: Man of Steel* #80 (June 1998), DC Comics.
20. Jon Bogdanove and Louise Simonson, *Superman: Man of Steel* #81 (July 1998), DC Comics.
21. Florida Center for Instructional Technology, "Mordechai Anielewicz," A Teacher's Guide to the Holocaust, http://fcit.usf.edu/holocaust/people/Anielewi.htm.

Chapter 2. Batman and the Spirit: Urban Darkness

1. Bob Kane, *Batman and Me* (Forestville, CA: Eclipse Books, 1989), 20.
2. Ibid., 2.
3. Bob Callahan, "Father of Urban Darkness," Salon.com, November 6, 1998, http://www.salon.com/news/1998/11/06newsc.html.
4. Kane, *Batman and Me*, 1.
5. Alan Oirich, "The Adventures of Batmensch," *Jewsweek*, August 3, 2005, http://www.jewsweek.com/bin/en.jsp?enDispWho=Article%5El1809&enPage=BlankPage&enDisplay=view&enDispWhat=object&enVersion=0&enZone=Stories&.
6. Bob Kane, *Detective Comics* #33 (November 1939), reprinted in *Batman: The Dark Knight Archives*, vol. 1 (New York: DC Comics, 1992), 11.
7. Eccles. 4:9–11.
8. Kane, *Batman and Me*, 101.
9. Quoted in Fran Nachman Putney, "Zap! Pow!" *Atlanta Jewish Times,* October 15, 2004.
10. Kane, *Batman and Me*, 152.
11. Rebecca Roiphe and Daniel Cooper, "Batman and the Jewish Question," *New York Times,* July 2, 1992.
12. Ben Macintyre, "Is Batman a Racist Bigot?" *Times* (London), August 4, 2002.
13. Bob Kane, "The 1,000 Secrets of the Batcave!" *Batman* #48, (August–September 1948), reprinted in *Batman: In the Forties* (New York: DC Comics, 2004), 84.
14. Callahan, "Father of Urban Darkness."
15. Quoted in Ken Quattro, "Rare Eisner: Making of a Genius," Comicartville Library http://www.comicartville.com/rareeisner.htm.
16. Quoted in Michael Barrier, "Will Eisner: Moved by the Spirit," Michael Barrier.com, http://www.michaelbarrier.com/Essays/Eisner/essay_Eisner.htm.
17. Quoted in Weiss, "Secret Identities."
18. Ibid.
19. Quoted in Julia Goldman, "The King of Comic Books" *Jewish Week*, May 31, 2002, http://www.thejewishweek.com/news/newscontent.php3?artid=6241.
20. Jules Feiffer, *The Great Comic Book Heroes* (New York: Fantagraphics, 2003), 39.
21. Quoted in Goldman, "The King of Comic Books."
22. Lev. 19:18.

23. Exod. 2:12.
24. Exod. 21:24.
25. *Ethics of the Fathers* 2:6.

Chapter 3. Captain America: Star-Spangled Salvation

1. Quoted in Weiss, "Secret Identities."
2. Quoted in Dan Whitehead, "KAPOW! A Talk with Joe Simon," Simon Entertainment Properties, http://www.simoncomics.com/jsmag.htm.
3. Quoted in Kaplan, "How Jews Created the Comic Book Industry, Part I."
4. Michael Chabon, *The Amazing Adventures of Kavalier and Clay* (New York: Picador USA, 2000).
5. Quoted in Weiss, "Secret Identities."
6. Joe Simon and Jack Kirby, "The Camera Fiend and His Darts of Doom," *Captain America Comics* #6 (September 1941), reprinted in *Captain America: The Classic Years*, vol. 2, #6 (New York: Marvel Comics, 2000).
7. Quoted in Michael Aushenker, "You Don't Know Jack: How Judaism Informed the Life and Art of a Legendary Cartoonist," *Jewish Journal of Greater Los Angeles*, August 24, 2001.
8. Quoted in Aushenker, "You Don't Know Jack."
9. R. C. Harvey, "If Jews Created Comics, Are Comics, Then, Jewish?" *Comic Book Marketplace* 3, no. 116 (October 2004): 20.
10. Quoted in Arie Kaplan, "Kings of Comics: How Jews Transformed the Comic Book Industry, Part I: The Golden Age (1933–1955)" *Reform Judaism*, Fall 2003.
11. Quoted in Ronin Ro, *Tales to Astonish* (New York: Bloomsbury USA, 2004), 21.
12. Quoted in Ro, *Tales to Astonish*, 35.
13. Jeet Heer, review of *The Comics Journal Library: Jack Kirby*, ed. Milo George and Stan Lee, *National Post*, October 11, 2003.

Chapter 4. The Justice League of America: A (Justice) League of their Own

1. Fredric Wertham, *Seduction of the Innocent* (New York: Rinehart & Company, 1954).
2. Wertham, *Seduction of the Innocent*, 15.
3. Julius Schwartz, *Man of Two Words* (New York: HarperCollins, 2000), 2.
4. Ibid., 5.
5. Ibid., 14.
6. Ibid., 69.
7. Ibid., 77.
8. Elliot S. Maggin, "Remembering Julius Schwartz," Superman.ws: The Superman Website, http://theages.superman.ws/julie/.
9. Gardner Fox and Mike Sekowsky, "Starro the Conqueror!" *The Brave and the Bold* #28 (February–March 1960), reprinted in *Justice League of America*, vol. 1, Archive Editions (New York: DC Comics, 1992), 14.
10. Deut. 16:20.

11. Exod. 17:8-13.
12. Gerard Jones and Chuck Wojtkiewicz, "Where the Wild Things Are," *Justice League of America* #95 (New York: DC Comics, January 1995).
13. Keith Giffen and Paul Levitz, "And the Sky Itself Shall Burn!" *Legion of Super-Heroes* #308 (February 1984), DC Comics.

Chapter 5. Fantastic Four: "F" for Dysfunctional

1. Stan Lee and George Mair, *Excelsior! The Amazing Life of Stan Lee* (New York: Fireside, 2002), 118.
2. Ibid., 5.
3. Stan Lee and Jack Kirby, "The Menace of the Miracle Man," *Fantastic Four* #3 (March 1962), reprinted in *Essential: The Fantastic Four*, vol. 1, #1–20 and Annual #1 (New York: Marvel Comics, 2005).
4. Stan Lee and Jack Kirby, "The Fantastic Four," *Fantastic Four* #1 (November 1961), reprinted in *Essential: The Fantastic Four*, vol. 1, #1–20 and Annual #1 (New York: Marvel Comics, 2005).
5. Lee and Mair, *Excelsior!* 117.
6. Edward S. Shapiro, *We Are Many: Reflections on American Jewish History and Identity* (Syracuse, NY: University Press, 2005), 106.
7. Karl Kesel and Stuart Immonen, "Remembrance of Things Past," *Fantastic Four*, vol. 3, #56 (August 2002), Marvel Comics.
8. Ibid.
9. Ibid.
10. Ibid.
11. Rambam, *Hilchos Mamrim* 3:3.
12. Kesel and Immonen, "Remembrance."
13. "The Jewish Thing," interview with Tom Brevoort and Stan Lee, *On the Media*, WNYC Radio, August 2, 2002, http://www.onthemedia.org/transcripts/transcripts_080202_thing.html.
14. Quoted in Ro, *Tales to Astonish*, 163.
15. "The Jewish Thing."
16. Quoted in Vince Beiser, "The Brainchildren of Stan Lee," *Jerusalem Report*, August 2005.
17. Quoted in Sheli Teitelbaum, "The Rise of Captain Marvel," *Jerusalem Report*, August 2005.

Chapter 6. The Incredible Hulk and Sabra: Anger Management

1. Lee and Mair, *Excelsior!* 120.
2. Stan Lee and Jack Kirby, "The Hulk," *The Incredible Hulk* #1 (May 1962), reprinted in *The Essential Hulk,* vol. 1, #1–6 (New York: Marvel Comics, 2005).
3. Stan Lee and Jack Kirby, "The Terror of the Toad Men," *The Incredible Hulk* #2 (July 1962), reprinted in *The Essential Hulk*, vol. 1, #1–6 (New York: Marvel Comics, 2005).
4. Lee and Mair, *Excelsior!* 121.

5. Ibid., 120.

6. Talmud, Sanhedrin 65b.

7. Chabon, *The Amazing Adventures of Kavalier and Clay.*

8. Quoted in Arie Kaplan, "How Jews Transformed the Comic Book Industry, Part II: The Silver Age (1956–1978)," *Reform Judaism*, Winter 2003, http://reformjudaismmag.net/03winter/comics.shtml.

9. Roy Thomas and Herb Trimpe, "Day of Thunder, Night of Death," *The Incredible Hulk* #133 (November 1970), reprinted in *The Essential Hulk,* vol. 3, #118–142, (New York: Marvel Comics, 2005).

10. Roy Thomas and Herb Trimpe, "Among Us Walks the Golem," *The Incredible Hulk* #134 (December 1970), reprinted in *The Essential Hulk,* vol. 3, #118–142, *Captain Marvel* #20–21, and *Avengers* #88 (New York: Marvel Comics, 2005).

11. Ibid.

12. Peter David, Dale Keown, and Sam Delarosa, "Mending Fences," *The Incredible Hulk,* vol.2, #373 (September 1990), Marvel Comics.

13. Rambam *Hilchos De'as Chap 2. Halacha 3.*

14. Bill Mantlo and Sal Buscema, "Power and Peril in the Promised Land," *The Incredible Hulk* #256 (February 1981), Marvel Comics.

15. Ibid.

16. Ibid.

17. Ibid.

18. Quoted in Mark Goldwert, "It's a Bird, It's a Plane—It's Sabra!" *New Jersey Jewish News*, July 7, 2002, http://www.juf.org/news_public _affairs/article.asp?key=3352.

19. Nick Taylor, "Giving the Female Character Sabra a Series of Her Own," PetitionOnline, http://www.petitiononline.com/123A/petition.html.

20. Michael Chabon, "Essay: A Woman of Valor," Organ: Collecting the Uncollected, March 2005, http://www.michaelchabon.com/ archives/2005/03/a_woman_of_valo.html.

21. Ibid.

Chapter 7. Spider-Man: "Wherever There's a Hangup . . ."

1. Lee and Mair, *Excelsior!* 126–127.

2. Ibid., 128.

3. Stan Lee and Steve Ditko, *Amazing Fantasy* #15 (August 1962), reprinted in *The Essential Spider-Man,* vol. 1, #1–20 (New York: Marvel Comics, 2004).

4. Ibid.

5. Ibid.

6. Quoted in Jeffrey Weiss, "Spider-Man's Balancing Act Resonates with Religious Leaders," *Lincon Journal Star*, July 17, 2004, http://www .journalstar.com/articles/2004/07/17/ values/10052472.prt.

7. John F. Kennedy, Inaugural Address, January 20, 1961, Bartleby Bookstore, http://www.bartleby.com/124/pres56.html.

8. Quoted in Sean Smith, "Along Came Spidey," *Newsweek*, June 28, 2005.

9. Quoted in Michael Aushenker, "Spider-Mensch: The Jewish Roots of

Director Sam Raimi and Spider-Man," *Jewish Journal of Greater Los Angeles*, April 26, 2002.

10. Danny Fingeroth, *Superman on the Couch: What Superheroes Really Tell Us about Ourselves and Society* (New York, London: Continuum), 75.
11. Quoted in Smith, "Along Came Spidey."
12. "Stan Lee: 'Insectman' Just Didn't Sound Right" interview by Kate Snow, CNN Access, May 4, 2002, http://edition.cnn.com/2002/SHOWBIZ/ Movies/05/04 /spiderman.stanlee.cnna.
13. Quoted in Aushenker, "Spider-Mensch."
14. "Raimi Hearts *Kavalier and Clay,*" *Word*, February 2005, reproduced on The Amazing Website of Kavalier and Clay, http://www.sugarbombs .com/kavalier/news2005feb.html.
15. Quoted in Kaplan, "How Jews Created the Comic Book Industry, Part I."
16. Stan Lee, telephone interview with the author, September 22, 2005.
17. Maimonides, "Mishneh Torah, Hilchot Mat'not Ani'im," 10:9.
18. Talmud, "Baba Batra," 9b.
19. J. Michael Straczynski and John Romita Jr, "You Want Pants with That?" *The Amazing Spider-Man*, vol. 2, #502 (New York: Marvel Comics, Feb. 2004).
20. Ibid.
21. Ibid.

Chapter 8. X-Men: Mutation Generation

1. Stan Lee and Jack Kirby, "X-Men," *X-Men* #1 (September 1963), reprinted in *Essential X-Men,* vol. 1, #1–24 (New York: Marvel Comics, 2003).
2. Stan Lee, "The Man behind Marvel Comics Ranks among the Jewish Pioneers of the Comic Book Industry," *Jewish Journal of Greater Los Angeles*, July 14, 2000.
3. Lee and Kirby, "X-Men."
4. Stan Lee and Jack Kirby, "The Brotherhood of Evil Mutants," *X-Men* #4 (March 1964), reprinted in *Essential: The Uncanny X-Men*, vol. 1, #1–24 (New York: Marvel Comics, 2003).
5. Quoted in Arie Kaplan, "Kings of Comics: How Jews Transformed the Comic Book Industry Part II: The Silver Age (1956–1978)" *Reform Judaism*, Winter 2003.
6. Ibid.
7. Chris Claremont and John Bolton, "I, Magneto," *Classic X-Men* #19 (March 1978) Marvel Comics.
8. Quoted in Kaplan, "Kings of Comics: Part II" *Reform Judaism*, Winter 2003.
9. Jim Lee and Chris Claremont, "Rubicon," *X-Men* vol. 2, #1 (October 1991), Marvel Comics.
10. Simon Wiesenthal, *Justice, Not Vengeance* (New York: Grove Weidenfeld, 1990).
11. Quoted in Michael Aushenker, "Minority Retort: Director Bryan Singer Deepens Themes of Persecution and Pogrom in the Sequel *X2: X-Men United*," *Jewish Journal of Greater Los Angeles*, May 1, 2003.

12. Quoted in Teitelbaum, "The Rise of Captain Marvel."
13. "Auschwitz: The Nazis & the 'Final Solution,'" press release, December 12, 2004, BBC Press Office, http://www.bbc.co.uk/pressoffice/pressreleases/stories/2004/12_december/02/auschwitz.shtml.
14. Rabbi Yaakov Kleiman, "The Cohanim/DNA Connection: The Fascinating Story of How DNA Studies Confirm an Ancient Biblical Tradition," Aish.com, http://www.aish.com/societywork/sciencenature/the_cohanim_-_dna_connection.asp.

Index

MORE FROM LEVIATHAN PRESS

JEWISH HERO CORPS #1:
The Amnesia Coutdown
Alan Oirich

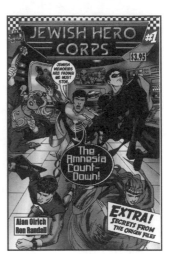

The Amnesia Countdown, the first issue of the *Jewish Hero Corps* comic book series, tells the story of the world's only Jewish superhero team as they go on a worldwide race against time to stem the tide of "Jewish Amnesia." Aside from providing a fast-paced action-adventure story, the new series strives to bolster a sense of Jewish identity and give the reader some basic Jewish knowledge.

Experience the holidays with Shimon Apisdorf

ROSH HASHANAH YOM KIPPUR SURVIVAL KIT
Shimon Apisdorf
Benjamin Franklin Award winner

There you are; it's the middle of High Holy Day services, and frankly, you're confused. Enter the *Rosh Hashanah Yom Kippur Survival Kit*. This book follows the order of the services and masterfully blends wisdom, humor, and down-to-earth spirituality. It's like having a knowledgeable friend sitting right next to you in synagogue.

FALL 2006: Look for the *Rosh Hashanah Yom Kippur Survival Kit* in Russian!

THE SURVIVAL KIT FAMILY HAGGADAH
Shimon Apisdorf

The only Haggadah in the world featuring the Matzahbrei Family, a loveable family of matzah people that guides you and your family through a delightful, insightful, spiritual, and fun seder. Featuring the "talking Haggadah" and a revolutionary translation. Never again will you read a paragraph in the Haggadah and say, "Huh, what's that supposed to mean?" This Haggadah is the perfect companion to *Judaism in a Nutshell: Passover*.

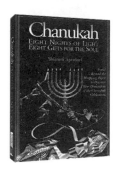

CHANUKAH: EIGHT NIGHTS OF LIGHT, EIGHT GIFTS FOR THE SOUL
Shimon Apisdorf
Benjamin Franklin Award winner

This book takes you way beyond the wrapping paper to discover a little-known spiritual dimension of Chanukah. From the lighting of the candles to the dreidel to the Maccabees, this book explores fascinating dimensions of the Chanukah celebration. Includes everything a family needs to experience, enjoy, and be inspired by the holiday.

THE ONE HOUR PURIM PRIMER
Shimon Apisdorf

This book has everything a family needs to understand, celebrate, and enjoy Purim. User-friendly. Packed with great ideas for adults and children. Also includes a complete Hebrew-English Megillah/Book of Esther with brief explanations and commentary.

The Jewish Cheat Sheet Series

HIGH HOLIDAY CHEAT SHEET

If you are one of those people who has a hard time finding meaning in the High Holidays, then you absolutely won't want to leave for synagogue without your High Holiday Cheat Sheet. This brochure-sized pocketful of inspiration provides insights into the holidays, thoughtful explanations of the traditions, and guides to the deeper meaning of some of the most important prayers.

HANUKKAH CHEAT SHEET

If one day's worth of oil burned for eight days, why can't you become a Hanukkah expert in just eight minutes? This Cheat Sheet has everything you need to become a veritible encyclopedia of Hanukkah knowledge and transform your experience of the holiday into a spiritually inspiring day.

PURIM CHEAT SHEET

This pamphlet is jam-packed with useful, fun, and practical information about the holiday of Purim, such as the story of Purim, some relevant Jewish history, inspiring and thought-provoking questions, a checklist of things to do before the holiday begins, and much more.

Coming Cheat Sheets: Israel Cheat Sheet
Sukkot Cheat Sheet

**THE BIBLE FOR THE CLUELESS
BUT CURIOUS: Finally, a Guide to Jewish
Wisdom for Real People**
Nachum Braverman
Benjamin Franklin Award winner

This is the award-winning book that launched the Clueless but Curious series. Maybe the last time you read the Bible was in Sunday School, or maybe you never read it at all. *The Bible for the Clueless but Curious* won't throw a bunch of "thous" and "forsooths" at you and won't try to make you feel guilty about anything. This book is for thoughtful people who have never had a chance to discover the world of wisdom in the Bible and see how it can actually be relevant to life in the 21st century. A cast of fun and friendly icons helps make this book a delightful read.

"Nachum Braverman is one of the most provocative and inspiring teachers in the Jewish world today."
—David Wilstein, past General Chairman, United Jewish Fund of Los Angeles; President, Realtech Leasing and Management

**KOSHER FOR THE CLUELESS
BUT CURIOUS: A Fun, Fact-Filled, and
Spiritual Guide to all Things Kosher**
Shimon Apisdorf

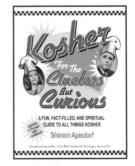

Kosher foods, kosher cooking, and the kosher dietary laws make up one of the most widely known yet least understood areas of Judaism and Jewish life. *Kosher for the Clueless but Curious* is the first book to ever present all aspects of kosher—including the kitchen sink—to readers who are filled with curiosity but are hungry for easy-to-understand information.

Includes a stunning 24-page full-color cookbook featuring recipes from two world-class chefs—Susie Fishbein, author of the best-selling *Kosher by Design* cookbook series, and Scott Sunshine, a veteran chef of the gourmet cooking industry.

"I have guided hundreds of people who have begun to explore the meaning of a kosher lifestyle. Kosher for the Clueless but Curious *is the book I have always wished was available. It's highly informative, inspiring, and eminently practical."*
—Rabbi Shlomo Porter, Director, Etz Chaim Center for Jewish Studies, Baltimore; National President, Association for Jewish Outreach Programs

Judaism in a Nutshell Series

FOR PEOPLE WHO ARE LONG ON CURIOSITY BUT SHORT ON TIME

Judaism in a Nutshell
GOD
Shimon Apisdorf
Judaism in a Nutshell
HOLIDAYS
Shimon Apisdorf
Judaism in a Nutshell
ISRAEL
Shimon Apisdorf
Judaism in a Nutshell
Passover
Shimon Apisdorf

Each one of these books presents just about everything you need to know about one of the pillars of Judaism.

"Apisdorf has a unique ability to communicate the practical wisdom of Judaism and show how it relates to everyday life."
—The Jerusalem Report

Other Titles You Will Enjoy

THE DEATH OF CUPID
Reclaiming the wisdom of love, dating, romance and marriage
Nachum Braverman & Shimon Apisdorf

THE DEATH OF CUPID: Reclaiming the Wisdom of Love, Dating, Romance, and Marriage
Nachum Braverman and Shimon Apisdorf

The Death of Cupid is divided into four sections: The Wisdom of Marriage, The Wisdom of Dating, The Wisdom of Sex, and The Wisdom of Romance. This book speaks equally to singles in search of love and to couples seeking to deepen their relationship.

REMEMBER MY SOUL: What To Do in Memory of a Loved One
Lori Palatnik

An informative, insightful, and practical guide to the Jewish understanding of death and mourning. The book includes a guided journey through shiva and the stages of Jewish mourning. While reading the book, readers also create a Diary of Remembrance that becomes a personal keepsake.

Remember My Soul
What To Do In Memory Of A Loved One

FALL 2006: Look for the revised and expanded edition of *Remember My Soul*

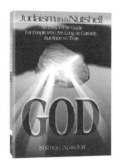

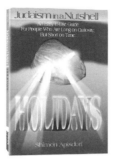

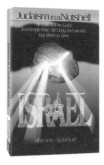

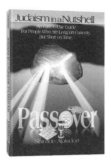

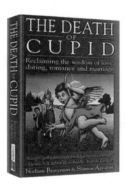

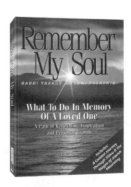

On the Leviathan Press Horizon

AT RISK BUT NOT BEYOND REACH: A Real World Guide to Understanding and Nurturing the Teenagers You Love
Rabbi Daniel Schonbuch

Teenagers are mystifying, lovable, and often terrifying. For parents and educators who are struggling to raise, nurture, teach, or guide a teenager, this book is a must. Presents a thoughtful, practical, tested, and easy to implement strategy.

A BEAUTIFUL BUSINESS IS A LIVING WORK OF ART
Dr. Paul Volosov

"Doing good for others and doing well for yourself and your family are perfectly compatible goals. All you need is to maintain a sense of priority. First meet the needs and wants of the customer. The money will follow." In this book, Paul Volosov, Ph.D., a very successful behavioral health entrepreneur, offers a new way of envisioning the meaning of business, a model for building businesses that not only do *well* but also do *good*, and a method to explore some of life's most important questions in the process.

THE YIZKOR COMPANION GUIDE
Lori Palatnik

The Yizkor ceremony is rich with opportunities for profound reflection and deep connection with a departed loved one. Lori Palatnik has created a beautiful, concise guide to Yizkor that helps people access the rich spiritual potential hidden within the Yizkor service.

THE ULTIMATE JEWISH TRAVELER'S GUIDE AND ALMANAC
Compiled by Jeffrey Seidel's Jewish Student Information Center

Absolutely everything the Jewish traveler needs to know: from little-known points of Jewish interest to kosher eateries, where to experience Shabbat in Bombay, whom to call in Brazil if you need a synagogue, and much more. This indispensable guide puts every bit of information that international Jewish travelers need right where they want it—at their fingertips.

Leviathan Press Order Information

TO ORDER:
Phone: 1-800-Leviathan (538-4284) or 410-653-0300
Email: orders@leviathanpress.com
Online: www.leviathanpress.com or www.jewishcheatsheets.com

NON-PROFIT BULK ORDERS
All of our products can be purchased at significant bulk order discounts by schools, synagogues, educational institutions, and other non-profit organizations. Cheat Sheets and many of our books can be customized to promote your organization. Contact us for special prices and customization options.

AND GOD CREATED THE GIANT SEA CREATURES . . .
Genesis 1:21

THESE SEA CREATURES WERE THE LEVIATHAN.
Talmud

THE LEVIATHAN REPRESENTS SOMETHING OF
"GIANT" SPIRITUAL POTENTIAL.
Maharal of Prague

The Leviathan is a mystical aquatic creature linked
to a realm of deep spiritual insight.
The Leviathan evokes the search for timeless ideas
as relevant today as they were eons ago.
Since 1992, Leviathan Press has brought rays of Jewish
wisdom and spirituality to the English-speaking public.

leviathan press™
wisdom for the mind, inspiration for the soul™

www.leviathanpress.com

About the Author

Simcha Weinstein holds a bachelor's degree in film history from Manchester Metropolitan University in England. Following graduation, he became a film and television location scout.

It is said that when man makes plans, God laughs. Following a major career turn, not to mention a life-altering paradigm shift, Simcha is now the rabbi of both Pratt Institute and Long Island College Hospital and the founder of the downtown Brooklyn Jewish Student Foundation, an educational and cultural center that strives to ignite Jewish pride and commitment through innovative educational and social experiences in an open environment.

Simcha is a witty, entertaining, and much sought-after public speaker. He is married with two children and lives in Brooklyn Heights, New York. You can reach Simcha at www.rabbisimcha.com or rabbisimcha@pratt.edu.